DEDICATION

To you! You've made it this far! Keep going for your dreams!

CONTENTS

What Is The Next Level

"I just feel kind of stuck…."

I hear people saying that all around the world right now. I just feel stuck. They're stuck in a job they don't want or a relationship they don't want and unfortunately it's not even that specific for some people. Some people just feel stuck in life.

Where does that come from? You'll remember in My Story that I told you in the ABC's of Success that I had that same feeling. I felt stuck. I had a job, a family, beautiful children, a house and what most people would consider a good life. But here was the problem. I wanted more. Not from a greedy, give it to me, frame of mind; I just knew something was missing. I spent a lot of time and money on personal growth, self-help, psychology, and even exploring various types of businesses that I thought would get me what I wanted. Believe me they all helped. Some of them helped me realize what I didn't want in my life and others helped me realize what I did want in my life or what I wanted more of in my life.

I've always been good at taking something that is complex and breaking it down into a simpler form. I enjoy simple. I think that if life is complicated that you aren't doing it right. I also think that if you aren't having fun you're definitely not doing life right. So in this book I wanted to put together what I learned from a psychology point of view and get in your head a little bit. I'm going to poke around a little bit up there. I might stir up some feelings. But, stay with me and you'll come out at the top a sturdier, wiser, more focused person. Now as we begin The Next Level I have some good news and I have some bad news.

The first thing that I want to do is tell you the bad news. The bad news is you have probably been here already. You might have been living at this level most of your life. So, unfortunately you already know how to get to this point in life. Most people have, most people live at this level. The good news is I'm going to show you why you've been stuck at this level and how you can break through and reach the peak. As soon as you can recognize the four things that are holding you back you will know exactly how to break through and get to any level you want. So if you are ready to learn that, let's get started.

The Next Level is more about the psychological aspects of your life and what stops you from reaching the peak. What is going to stop you from reaching higher than you have ever reached before and living a life that you have never lived before? You might say, "Maybe it's possible for other people but I don't know if it's possible for me." I'm telling you that it is. Again, trust the process of getting there.

I've shown you exactly how to achieve your goals, both large and small. They are exactly the same. You practice the ABC's of Success which you learned in the first book. You follow the pattern of 'be, do, have', you recognize your associations, you use your time management skills and put the smack down on those goals. You do all the things that we learned about in Your Journey Of Being - The ABC's of Success. It's important that you understand all of those lessons in the ABC's of Success before you start The Next Level. I'm hoping you do, but if you don't, you can always review the first book and then continue with The Next Level at any time. In order to increase the size of the goal, you just increase the size of the pattern, it's all the same. Whether you want to set a goal to lose twenty pounds or to lose two hundred pounds, the process is the same, you just increase the size of the pattern. Here is how the pattern looks.

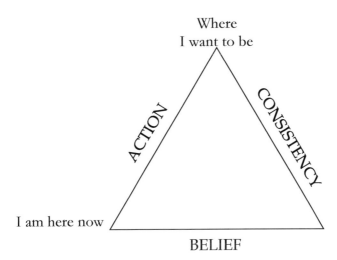

Everything, no matter what goal you want to achieve, is going to be based on what you learned in the ABC's of Success, and that's going to be your foundation for this section. This Next Level is going to increase the awareness of what is happening in your own mind. When you increase the awareness of what is in your own mind, your ability to see the world in a whole new way is going to be amazing. You're going to learn how you think and you're going to learn how other people think. You're even going to discover the ability to read people's minds!

Not really. You actually already know that apparently and I'm going to show you why. Human beings think and act in similar ways. Sure, we all do things differently, we all think different thoughts, but in general, human beings are pretty similar. Obviously some people think at higher levels, some people think at very low levels and some people don't think at all. I'm just kidding of course, but some people don't really use the knowledge they have in order to live the life they want. So by learning how to master your own thoughts, you can in fact master how to use your mind so you can achieve any goal. What is even more beneficial is, you can begin to influence other people to help you achieve your goals and help you create and live the exact life that you want. Now won't that be cool.

Won't it be really cool when you are able to look at people and influence the way they behave with mind control techniques. Okay, don't get your hopes up, it's not exactly like that, but you are going to be able to influence people. You are going to use what you know to your advantage when you are done with this book and that's going to be a really cool way for you to live. So stay tuned for that and more.

What are you going to learn in The Next Level? The primary focus in The Next Level is identifying what's going to stop you. Wouldn't it be nice if you knew what was going to stop you before you even started so that when something did get in your way you could just blast through it and never let it slow you down? Well, that is what we are going to focus on as a general premise of this entire section. We're going to build upon the foundation that you learned in the ABC's of Success and we're going to focus on moving past this place where most people settle in and live life. It's where you may be living and unfortunately most people never reach the peak. So I'm going to show you how to get to the peak, live there, and create your life in that space. But first I have to teach you how to break through the four things that are going to stop you.

We are going to build on that foundation. We are going to continue to use goal setting and the achievement principles that you learned in the ABC's of Success, along with what you will learn in The Next Level. We are going to progressively build. This series of books is a step by step guide, containing everything you need to learn to live a life you love. Eventually, once you are done with this entire series, you are going to live life at your peak at every moment, of every day! At least that is my goal for you. I can't force you to live there but I'm telling you it is an amazing place. I'm going to show you how to get there and it's up to you to make the choice to live there or not, fair enough?

Much like you learned in the ABC's of Success, there are some pretty predictable patterns for happiness and success. Remember, I mentioned there are going to be four things that are going to attempt to stop you. That's it, just four things that stand in your way, every single time that you want to live at another level. When you realize what those four things are and you are able to break through them consistently, you'll be able to reach your goals much more quickly. Each journey is going to take you a different amount of time, depending on the size of the goal. But every journey begins and ends the same way every time.

I'm going to give you the road map. Where you are now and where you want to be is only separated by everything you are going to learn in this series of books. Once you learn to master the information in this book, you learn to master life itself. The first thing I want to do is talk about the definition of life coaching. To me, life coaching is a practice. It's a practice of observing your patterns, identifying the hidden, self-imposed barriers that stop you from reaching your goals, and recognizing those patterns and barriers.

Once we discover those patterns, effective coaching consists of developing specific goals and showing you how to be self-confident in identifying those barriers and helping you blast through them without the assistance of a coach. Think of this book as me, coaching you, so that you can blast through your hidden self-imposed barriers. Whether they are external barriers or internal barriers, either way, my goal is to give you everything you need to reach any level of happiness and success that you desire. However, I called this a practice because that is what this is. Like anything else that you want to master, practice is the key.

This section is all about identifying those hidden, self imposed barriers to your success, and again, there are only four of them. Identifying those barriers is just one aspect. Breaking through those barriers is another. I'm going to show you how to crush those barriers like they never even existed. I am hoping, if I do my job well, that you will break through those barriers and live at your peak every single day of your life. That's what I want for you. What lies at the other side of those barriers that we are going to identify in The Next Level, is your peak. When people talk about peak performance and living at your peak, which is really what we are talking about, you will be living at a level that you have never consistently lived at before.

But that's later, for now let's concentrate on breaking through those barriers. Much like the ABC's of Success, whatever goal you want to accomplish, whether it is a small goal, a big goal, or a world changing goal, all of that is going to become achievable to you. In fact, whatever you want for your life is possible, anything.

However, you must participate in order for that to happen. You can't just lie down and read this and say, "Give it to me." You've got to be doing the work as it's designed to be done. If you don't, you're not going to know what you are missing out on. You can read this, you can get information, and you can certainly grow as a human being learning everything I have to teach you here but if you do the work, your level of success will be so much greater. Your ability to understand and achieve and reach those new levels of success, no matter what they are in your life, are going to come to you and be so much clearer to you if you actually participate and do the work. Complete the work in this book as if it is the thing that can totally transform your life. I want you to trust this process, participate, openly give of yourself, and be one hundred percent honest with your answers.

What are you going to learn? First, we are going to recognize those challenges you are going to face but we are going to focus on the solutions to those challenges. We are going to identify what has stopped you in the past but we are going to focus on moving forward. We are going to foresee obstacles that may get in your way but we are going to focus on breaking through those barriers that may stand in your way. We are going to identify your stories but we are going to focus on what really happens. We are going to desire results in your life but we are going to focus on making progress. We are going to envision what's possible for your life but we are going to focus on making possibilities a reality. Yes, we are going to focus a lot in this book.

What's Your Story?

The first thing we are going to focus on is how your thoughts influence your life. You learned in the ABC's of Success that your thoughts really are your beliefs. Your thoughts are what determine what you can achieve. We are going to go deeper into that right now. Our thoughts and beliefs are shaped over time. They are the culmination of every individual life event and more importantly, how you viewed those events. Each and every one of us view our lives through a lens and that lens is our belief system. We only allow through what we believe. Our lens is the filter from which we make up the story that is our life.

Your story, as it would be told by you, if you were to write down everything that ever happened to you in your own words from your own viewpoint, would be a complete fabrication of reality. It would be a story, based on your perspective of the actual events of your life and how they would look on camera. It would be your perception of what you think happened in your life. Now, of course, everyone views life from how they see it. Everybody has their own thoughts and those thoughts are their belief system. So they view life and what happens to them by their belief system. So you have to understand that your life and your story is a fabrication of what you allow through your lens and that lens is your belief system.

A camera has a lens but it doesn't filter. The lens on a camera allows what is in front of it to come in. So what you view through the lens of your belief system, what you allow in, is going to be different from what really happens. This is an important element of what we are going to be covering here in The Next Level, because when we add in our own thoughts, feelings, beliefs and emotions, with what really happened, that is when we create a story. When you do this, at that very moment, you create a story from your perception of what you think happened. So every time you tell yourself a story of what you think happened, it's a thought based on your belief system, which is based on your perception of what you think happened.

That's all it is and that's a story that you tell yourself over and over and over again. People do it all day long, every day. Once you become aware that your life is a story everything will change for you, I promise you that. There is a pattern I want you to recognize in how your life goes. This happens 24 hours a day, 7 days a week for your entire life. It will not change. The pattern goes like this. Your thoughts happen in your life 24 hours a day. Every moment of your life you are having thoughts. They are conscious and subconscious. That inner voice that is running in your head is a thought stream. Some of those thoughts are just subconscious thoughts that are never more than subconscious. You filter those out and your brain does this on purpose. There is, again, scientific ways of understanding how all of that works but for this, as long as you know that your thoughts are running in your head 24 hours a day, all the time, at every moment of your life that is what you need to know. The thoughts that make their way from your subconscious to your conscious are what you experience as 'the voice.'

Now, those thoughts create an emotion within you. So, if your thought is, "I can't do this," the emotion is going to be one of discouragement. If your thought is, "I can do that, no problem," your emotion is going to be one of encouragement. Your thoughts always determine your emotions and sometimes your thoughts aren't even conscious. Subconscious thoughts are always going on, constantly streaming, every moment of every day, you can't stop that, it just happens. They play a tremendous role in your underlying view of life, but they don't develop into emotions. However, every thought that becomes a conscious thought does create an emotion.

Those emotions that you have, based on the thoughts that you have are going to create an action and sometimes they create inaction. So the conscious thoughts that create emotions begin to create an action that you take or do not take. So, if your thought is, "I can't do that," and your emotions is one of discouragement, then your inaction might be to just sit on the couch. On the other hand, if your thought is, "I can do that with no problem," your emotions is encouragement, and your action would be to do what you need to do to accomplish the goal.

Finally, your actions create your results. So your thoughts, feelings, and actions create your results. Again, the pattern continues, thought, "I can't do that," feeling of discouragement, action (or inaction) of sitting on the couch, result is nothing changes. Now, the other way, your thought is "I can do that," feeling is encouragement, action is to do what is necessary, and the result is you get what you want.

Thought, emotion, action, result. Everything that happens in your life is a result of that pattern. Those thoughts are that little voice in your head. That voice is continually going. It's like a little guy who just won't shut up. He is constantly talking, over, and over, and over again. That voice continues to tell us what we like and what we don't like. That voice tells us what we know and what we don't know. That voice tells us what is possible and what is not possible, what looks good and doesn't look good, what tastes good and doesn't taste good, what smells good and what doesn't smell good. It tells us everything all day long.

You are probably aware of that little voice. It is the same voice that sings a song to you over and over again so you can't stop listening to it. It's the same voice that you laugh at if you think a funny thought in your head. It's the same voice that you use to pray, if you do pray. That little voice is living in your head. Now, I'm probably not telling you anything new here, but I really want you to be aware of that voice. I want you to be more aware of it then you have ever been in your entire life. You don't have to pay one hundred percent attention to that voice all the time because that would drive you insane.

That voice is your voice. I've got to tell you, unfortunately, you are stuck with that voice. That is your voice and you can't get rid of it so you need to learn how to control that voice. From now on you need to be acutely aware of what that voice is saying. You have to be mindful of the fact that your voice is the greatest story teller in the entire world. That voice tells true stories. That voice tells fictional stories, that voice narrates our lives, that voice sings to us and supposedly that voice can even read the minds of other people.

Do you think I'm kidding that your inner voice reads the minds of other people? Well think of a time when you've had a conversation, perhaps even an argument, in your own head, and the other person that you were having a conversation with wasn't even in the same room. If they were in the same room, they weren't actually talking, you were just reading their mind apparently. You were going back and forth. You were saying in your head what you think they are going to say. You might have even been angry, having an all out argument with this person and they weren't even saying anything. Your inner voice spoke for that person. Your inner voice anticipated what you thought they were going to say. That inner voice even argued on their behalf. The inner voice that was speaking for the other person probably made you feel an emotion. That is a powerful voice to be able to do that to you, and we all do it. We are going to continue to do that forever, so the best thing you can do is to learn how to calm that voice.

I'm not here to tell you how you can stop the voice. But I am here to tell you that you do not, unless you have some magical ability, you do not have the ability to know exactly what someone else is thinking, what they will say, or anything else that is in that person's head. You need to understand that you are not a mind reader. You can't stop your inner voice but you can become aware that your inner voice is basically a psychotic, evil, pathological liar that is out to destroy your life. Okay, maybe not, but the reality is, that voice is there. That voice is a liar. That voice loves to tell you lie after lie after lie, and it loves to make up stories. It might not be out to ruin your life but if you let it, it will. If you let your story control your life, if you let that voice tell you a story and you live in that story, it can in fact destroy your life. Now I am going to teach you why.

Tell your story?

We're going to do a fill in the blank exercise now. I'll give you an example of how this might read, but you will need to write your own story. Yes, this is one chapter in my story of life.

"I have been telling myself that I <u>am never going to succeed at owning my own business.</u>

But that is a lie and I am going to overcome this negative disbelief with the belief that I am <u>on the right path and these failures are meant to be learning experiences to help me grow.</u>

<u>I have failed a lot in the past</u> and I have been making it mean <u>that I am never going to be as successful as I want to be and I should just settle for a "good life."</u>

Since I know that's a story, I am going to clear it up by allowing myself to accept <u>the fact that I was focused on the wrong type of business for the wrong reasons.</u>

I will acknowledge that I wasn't living with integrity for who I am committed to be by <u>focusing only on making money without being true to my core values as a person.</u>

I am recommitting to be who I was born to be and declaring that I am going to <u>follow my heart and live with purpose, based on my values and stop focusing on just making money.</u>

Okay, now it's your turn. Please fill in the blanks and begin to write the next chapter of your life.

My Old Story

I have been telling myself that I

_____

_____.

But that is a lie and I am going to overcome this negative disbelief with the belief that I am

_____

_____.

_____

and I have been making it mean

_____

_____.

Since I know that's a story, I am going to clear it up by allowing myself to accept

_____

_____.

I will acknowledge that I wasn't living with integrity for who I am committed to be by

_____

_____.

I am recommitting to be who I was born to be and declaring that I am going to

_____

_____.

Who Is Living In Your Head?

So who is that voice and why is it there? Well, that voice is you, that voice is your thoughts. That voice is also your parents, your friends, your teachers, the music you listen to, the shows you watch on television, the books you read, the internet sites you visit, everything you do, and say, and hear, and eat, and feel and experience in your life creates that voice. So that's what it is. That voice is the culmination of everything you have ever heard, seen, or come in contact with coupled with the thoughts that you have about each experience. The thoughts that you have about what you see, hear, or come in contact with become your story.

Those stories are a fabrication of actual events. If you were to look at the events on camera from every perspective and somehow had the ability to think back to what you were thinking at every moment of your life, you might start to think that your voice is clinically insane. Most of us can control that voice on some level. What is important to understand though is that your voice has no bearing on actual reality. It has no bearing on what really happens in your life. You might be saying to yourself, it's my voice, shouldn't I be listening to it, shouldn't I believe in it, shouldn't I follow that voice? The answer is yes and no. The point of becoming aware of that voice is so we can go to work learning how to control and use that voice to your advantage.

I'm going to guess, and as you go through The Next Level, you are probably going to see how that voice has been controlling you. Now, remember what one of our focuses was going to be when we went over what we were going to cover in The Next Level. We said that we were going to identify your stories and we are going to focus on what really happened. We are going to focus in The Next Level, on the truth. What is the truth of your life? What really happens in your life?

You have to understand that many times your thoughts, that little voice and that story is a complete work of fiction. Remember, the voice in your head is the greatest story teller in the world. If you don't understand what I am talking about with the stories and how we make up things, don't worry. Right now all you need to do is be perfectly clear about the fact that you do, in fact, have a voice in your head. I am confident that everyone reading this book has that awareness. I'm sure you are aware that you have a voice in your head. So if you are aware of it, then that awareness is all you need. From this point on I just want you to become more aware of that voice because that voice is going to be the greatest tool that you have in your ability to achieve your goals and live the life you want. If you are one of those people who just thought to yourself "I don't have that voice" then guess what… you just heard the voice.

I want you to imagine something for me. I want you to imagine that you are walking down the street and you are having a great day. The sun is shining and you are using what you learned in the ABC's of Success. You are living in the moment, and hopeful about your future. You are really appreciating what is going on around you. You are thinking about how great it will be when you achieve your goals. In fact you are on your way to accomplish one of those goals right now. All of a sudden, out of nowhere, this little ugly man pops out from the shadows. Where did he come from? You didn't even see where this guy came out from and he begins shouting some horrible, insulting words at you that are the complete opposite of what you were just thinking. He's telling you that you are stupid, that you can't do anything right, why are you even trying to change your life, you're never going to do it! He is insulting you right to your face. He spits at you, he points and laughs at you and he stands there waiting for you to do or say something back to him.

Oh, that sucks, where did this guy come from? But there you are, you stand there and you just take it. You don't do anything about it. You stand there continuing to allow this little man to insult you right to your face. He is saying horrible, awful things to you. He is, in modern terms, dissing you. He is disrespecting you and you are doing nothing to stop him. He's looking at you, daring you to challenge him, with this smug little look. It's like he is just daring you to say something back to him, but you don't. You're stuck. You don't move. You don't say or do anything. You just stand there.

Everyone around you is looking at you and they are looking in disbelief. They can't believe that you aren't doing anything. They know, and you know, that you can put the smack down on this little man but you don't do anything. You choose to stand there and take it. You allow this little man, this ugly, dirty, nasty man that's insulting you and spitting on you and telling you nasty, horrible things to ruin your day. In fact, you never get over that event. From that day on in your life, you relive that event over and over and over again in your head. You can't get past it and it's just running over and over again in your mind. You give up on your goals and you never got to where you wanted to be that day. You believed what he said and you allowed him to influence you and you chose to give up on your goals.

Would you ever let that happen to you? Would you ever let some, gross, dirty, little man walk up to you, insult your ability, tell you that you can't do something, spit at you, laugh at you and stand there challenging you to do something or say something to him and not say or do anything? I certainly hope not. But, that is what you do when you allow your disempowering thoughts to control your life. It is like you are letting that little man 'diss' you. He is disrespecting you. He is allowing you to live in *negative disbelief.*

I hope that in real life you would never let anyone treat you like that. So why are you allowing your own inner voice to treat you like that? Now, of course, this is a very vivid, exaggerated example of what your inner voice could say to you. I hope that you are not beating yourself up that badly. But a lot of people do say very disempowering things to themselves. They 'diss' themselves every day with their thoughts. They say, "I can't do it. I always mess that up. I don't deserve to live such a good life." Those are negative disbeliefs. Your negative thoughts are like that really annoying little man that shows up unexpectedly, and he insults you right to your face, for his own amusement. Then he stands there challenging you to defeat him. When that happens, when that little annoying man shows up, you need to put an immediate stop to his tormenting.

I'm going to give you a weapon, a weapon like no other weapon in the world. This weapon is the most vicious weapon that you can use against this little man. It literally has the ability to disintegrate him on contact. He will completely disappear, but the little man has a magic ability as well. When he disappears he can show up again any time he wants. The good news is that the weapon I am going to give you can also be replenished any time you want. So what is that weapon? That weapon is the cleanest bucket of water that you have ever seen in your life. That's right, like the witch in the Wizard of Oz, remember how the witch melts when Dorothy splashes water on her face, that's what happens to this little man when you take this bucket of water and splash it on him. He disintegrates.

In fact the label on the bucket reads…warning: disintegrates annoying little men on contact. So how do you use it? How do you use this weapon? It's simple. When that annoying little man shows up and begins to insult you and tell you that you can't do something, you simply open your head up, take out your brain, scrub it clean in that bucket of water, put your brain back in, and you close your head back up.

Now that doesn't make any sense right. Wouldn't you want to splash it on that little man? Aren't you supposed to take that bucket of water and splash that little man so he disintegrates? Absolutely, but where does that little man really live? That little man only exists in your mind, so in order to get to him, we need to brainwash you. We need to take that bucket of water and scrub your brain, clean. We need to brainwash you so you can get rid of that little guy. That little man who tells you disempowering things is not really there. You need to recognize that it's a story. It's all made up.

What are some possible things that voice can say to you? The voice of that little man that is stuck in your head might say to you, "You don't have the right skills to do that, you've never done it before, what makes you think you are going to do it now, you shouldn't even try it, you can't do it, give up…." Splash! You splash that water right in your own face, open up your head and scrub those thoughts right out with that pure, clear, gorgeous, clean water. You need to immediately brainwash yourself when that little man shows up.

Remember, your beliefs, which are your thoughts, have a direct result on your ability. We learned about this in the ABC's of Success. Your mind doesn't know the difference between what is real and what you tell it. So if you have a little voice telling you that you can't do things, that it's not possible, don't even try, you're stupid, you can't be loved, you can't do that and so on. If that little man is running around constantly telling your brain things like that, and you are not fighting off that little man, then what is your brain going to believe? Your brain is going to believe what it is told and it is going to go to work making that happen.

People constantly tell themselves what they think are harmless thoughts. They allow those thoughts to run over and over again in their heads. But, remember the pattern; a thought controls your feelings and those feelings determine the actions that you take and those actions determine the results. So you need to begin recognizing immediately when your inner voice, when that little man, is saying something disempowering to you. If it is a negative disbelief, you need to consciously override that with an empowering thought, and turn it into an empowering belief. Since your brain doesn't actually know the difference, wouldn't you want it to believe empowering thoughts?

Don't you want your brain to believe that you are capable, have the ability and that you are powerful beyond what you even believe is possible? Wouldn't you want your brain to believe that you are smart, you're funny, you're sexy, you lose weight easily and you can do anything that you want to do. Isn't it better to believe that you can create any possibility you want to create for yourself, and you can live any life you can envision? You have the ability to envision that life, to get there and to live there and to make that your reality. Don't you want to believe that? So why are you allowing that little man to say otherwise?

You might still find yourself, even though I have given you that bucket of water, you might find yourself face to face with that little man. You might find yourself listening to him constantly tell you those nasty things, but guess what, eventually that little man is going to get tired of being splashed in the face with a bucket of water. Unfortunately, he will never actually go away. You can't really get rid of that little man. It is always possible for that little man to reappear. Remember that is his magic ability. That is the power he has over you. You have an amazing weapon with that bucket of water and you can use that weapon to brainwash yourself and scrub him out of there but he can reappear at any moment. So you need to be sure that you keep your bucket full.

The good news is that you can reprogram that little voice. You can influence that little voice the same way that you can influence anyone else in the world. You can influence that little voice to say different things to you because you are going to teach that little voice to think differently. You are going to teach that little man how to say nice things. You are going to teach that little man how to be kind, how to love you.

Isn't it great that we can do that for ourselves? Since that little man lives in your brain, you can reprogram him. You can reprogram your brain. You can reprogram that little man and you can reprogram his voice. So imagine in the future if all you heard were positive, empowering, success reinforcement thoughts that made you feel strong and able to accomplish anything that you want to accomplish. Imagine if that little man is always popping up and saying, "Hey, great job, you can do it, you're the best, I love you, you're fantastic, I told you that you could do it, you're amazing, go for it!" Wouldn't it be nice if the little man said that! Well, of course it would. No one wants to be insulted and told negative things. So we are going to retrain that little man.

By this point, you probably realize that the bucket of water I'm talking about, isn't a literal bucket of water. The water is a metaphor that represents the new, fresh, clean, empowering thoughts you need to develop. So you keep your bucket full by continuing to read books like this, and other personal development books, videos, and audios that develop your mind into the type of mind that only thinks positive, motivated, and inspired thoughts all the time. Sorry, that's not going to happen, you'll forever have that negative voice, but as long as you keep your bucket full, you'll keep him from staying around too long. The point is to refocus, retrain, and reprogram your voice by listening to other voices that begin to solidify the belief system you want, so you can build upon that new belief system.

Brainwashing

Now brainwashing is a process. It is a process of taking the beliefs in that brain of yours and changing them through repetitious programming. You have already been brainwashing yourself your whole life. You have already been doing it for years now. The problem is you have been using warm, dirty water, which like a pig, is exactly where that little man loves to be. That little man loves to live in that muddy, filthy, nastiness which is your negative thoughts. Most of your inner self talk, unfortunately, is negative until you make the choice to change your negative self talk into positive self talk. We talked about using affirmations and "I am" statements to do that in The ABC's of Success. This can and will happen even more powerfully if you apply the techniques that we are going to cover here in The Next Level.

Remember, you have been brainwashing yourself for how many years? So how long do you think it will take you to scrub all of those thoughts out of your brain? It might not happen overnight. It might take you quite a while to use that clean, pure water to your advantage. It might take some elbow grease and a real hard scrubbing to get that little man to change the way he is thinking, to change your brain and to reprogram your mind. The good news is that once you begin to learn to use positive self talk to your advantage, the effect and the influence it is going to have on your life is going to be far greater than any negative thoughts that you ever had in your life.

So how do you do that? How do you change your thoughts? The first thing you have to do is to become very, very aware when negative thoughts pop into your head. As soon as that little man pops up and starts to say something negative, you need to stop it, throw the water in his face, and get him to disintegrate. As soon as you can start to do that immediately when you recognize what's happening, that is when you will be able to start to reprogram your brain much faster. You might find that you have been sitting there for ten minutes telling yourself negative disbelief after negative disbelief. You might find yourself sitting there thinking those thoughts and it might take you a little while to say, "Wait a second, that little man is back." You have to grab your bucket of water, splash him and make him disappear.

Sometimes he doesn't yell, sometimes he whispers. He whispers right in your ear and you can hardly hear him but it is enough for your subconscious mind to hear it and believe it. You don't have to be yelled at to hear negative things. Those negative thoughts might come in a form of a book or music or television or social media or anything else that you are exposed to on a regular basis. Remember, that little voice is everything around you. That little voice comes from what you are exposed to in your everyday life. So I'm not saying that you are always going to hear a blaring, negative thought in your head. When you start to see negative things happening and you start to experience a negative thought you are going to learn how to say, "Wait a second, I don't want that in my head," and you can use that bucket of water to scrub those thoughts out of your head. That might take turning off that program that you don't want to watch any more, or not listening to the person that you don't want to listen to any more, and not reading the blog or the social media posts that you don't want in your head. You have to use that bucket of water before anything around you has a chance to diss you. Before anything around you has a chance to disrespect the way you want to think.

Remember, negative thoughts create negative disbeliefs. They are disrespectful beliefs. What you really need to be aware of is who allows those negative disbeliefs to become your solidified belief system. You do! You allow negative disbeliefs into your life if you choose to. I'm hoping that you don't allow too much negative disbelief into your life in the future. I'm hoping that as much as possible you only allow positive beliefs into your life.

But that is going to take work, and practice, and time. It's also not likely that you'll never again have to struggle and fight to overcome those negative disbeliefs, because, they will be there. However, the better you get at putting this work into action the more often you will experience life at a new level of consciousness. That is what I want for you more than anything else. To experience what life can be like, living at the peak, every moment of your life.

I wish that we had the ability, like the sci-fi movies to put a program in your brain and reprogram every negative thought and create a positive thought instead. But unfortunately we don't have that ability yet so what we are going to use is good old fashioned positive reinforcement. Being more self aware, and being able to listen to your own inner voice and stopping it from telling you negative disbeliefs is a skill you are going to develop over time. More importantly, once your self awareness is heightened, we are going to start to control that inner voice. You're going to recognize when that little man is lying to you and you are going to see exactly how your thoughts are nothing more than just a story. You will be able to overcome those negative disbeliefs very quickly. This is a very, very powerful skill to develop for yourself and a very powerful skill in creating the life that you want. Overcoming those negative disbeliefs in your life is what is going to make or break your ability to live at your peak.

The first negative disbelief that you need to wipe clean out of your mind, to scrub out of there, is that things aren't possible. You need to know and believe that anything is possible. In your life, if you want something, you need to believe that it's possible. So if you find yourself saying, "That's not possible," scrub it out, get rid of it, brainwash it, even if it seems completely illogical, inconceivable, and unable to be accomplished, believe that anything is possible. So any time you find yourself saying, "That's not possible," stop the thought, scrub it out and get rid of it. In order to live the life that you want to live, you need to really create the thought and believe with all your heart that anything is possible.

As an example, imagine we're back in the year 1950. You and I are standing in a field talking while we work. You look at me and say, "I wish I could see and talk to my family, who are still on the other side of the world, but I had to move here to create a better life for myself." I look back at you and say, "Well, it is possible, maybe not right now, at this moment, but some day in the future it will be possible to stand in this very field, and see and talk to your family as if they were right here with you." You look at me and say "That's not possible." Yet I go on to spend my life working on creating the technology that allows us to video chat. I make a fortune and a huge difference in the world because I believed it was possible. Was it possible then? Yes, we just hadn't created the tools and technology yet, but it was in fact still possible!

We need to do that from this point on with consistent brainwashing. We need to brainwash you to believe anything that you want to believe. This is a very important factor for the law of attraction to work in your favor. The law of attraction states that the universe will make available to you, in abundance, what you are perfectly clear about in your intentions, and focus on long enough to allow the laws of the universe to attract together to provide it for you. So if you don't believe that having an abundance of love is possible then you won't have that in your life. If you don't believe that having an abundance of money is possible, you won't have that in your life. The universe provides for you only what you believe is possible.

This happens both positively and negatively so if your thoughts are consistently negative and you are allowing yourself to listen to that little man and his disbeliefs well then the universe uses its power to create that reality for you. The same goes for the positives. If you allow yourself to believe that anything is possible and you are thankful for everything that the universe has given you then the universe continues to make that possible for you. That's the way that the law of attraction works. That is the same way your brain works. Your brain works very similar to the law of attraction but your brain works much faster. The universal law of attraction takes time, your brain is immediate.

In order for the universe and the law of attraction to work you need to allow the universe time to make it happen. Most people fail to see the law of attraction and it's power at work because they don't give it enough time. They give up on their goals too quickly and they stop telling the universe what they want. So the universe had put some things in place but you didn't give it enough time to give you exactly what you want or you just weren't open to the opportunity. You have to make the choice to be open. Most people, ask for something, lose patience, and during that time that little man sneaks back in and begins to tell them that the law of attraction doesn't work. So don't allow that little man to show up in your life.

We are going to practice brainwashing throughout the rest of this course. For now, be aware of that little man who is going to show up from time to time and when he does, throw water in his face by telling him positive, motivational, empowering thoughts that you want him to believe. He will disappear for a while but be aware that he will try to sneak back in.

Become a D Student

Unfortunately, goal setting is not something that is taught in a traditional mainstream education, especially at this level. Most people never learned how to set goals. In the ABC's of Success you learned how to put the smack down on your goals, right? You learned that you need to be specific, motivated, achieving daily, committed to your goals, and you know that you have to keep going in order to reach the goal.

In this section we are going to focus more on the psychological aspects of achieving your goals. But don't lose site of the fundamentals. Writing down a specific goal and using a motivational reason why you want to complete that specific goal, achieving the steps, taking action, and receiving results are really important. Committing to your goals is really important. I'm going to show you goal setting and goal achieving at a whole new level. You are going to be required in this lesson to be a 'D' student. Can you do that for me? Can you be a 'D' student in goal setting and goal achieving? Well, of course I want you to be an 'A' student, I want you to be a Master at goal achievement. What I am saying is there are some D words that are going to help you to remember how to achieve your goals at a whole new level.

We are going to start with the D word of desire. In order for you to want to achieve anything in your life you have to have a desire to do it. I can tell you to go lift a truck but if you don't have the desire are you going to figure out how to get it done? No, if it doesn't matter to you, if it's not important to you well then why would you want to do it? But if your child were trapped underneath that truck, your desire would change. Whatever goals you want to achieve, you need to first start with the desire to accomplish that goal. Desire starts in your mind as a sense of longing for something.

Once you have the desire you really have to look at that goal and do the next D. In order to achieve your goals and have the commitment that it takes to continue to keep going when times get tough, you need to get disgusted. You have to look at that goal and get so disgusted by the fact that you haven't reached that goal yet, that you feel sick. Remember, I told you my story and how I got really disgusted by the fact that I realized that I could leave this earth and not leave this information for my kids. That was disgusting to me, it really upset me. So the second 'D' I want you to practice is getting disgusted. Don't stay disgusted, you're not disgusted with yourself. You are disgusted with the idea of not doing whatever it is that you really have a desire to do and you are motivated to do in your lifetime. So get disgusted. Use that emotion to take action and get into momentum.

Once you get disgusted, you are going to do the third D. You are going to decide to make a change. You'll see examples of this play out when you see drug addicts, alcoholics, or people with other addictive behavior scenarios hit rock bottom. The people who hit rock bottom experience a desire to make a change. Deep down inside they have the desire to make a change. A lot of times they just don't know how to make that change. Then once they hit rock bottom, they get disgusted. They get disgusted with their situation and with themselves and what their lives have become. Then they decide to make a change. At the moment they decide to make a change there is a shift in their thinking. There is a shift in how they view what's possible for their future. It might be scary but there is a glimmer of hope. When you decide to do something about your goals you will see a glimmer of hope. So decide that you are ready to make a change in your life based on the things that you are disgusted with because you have a desire to do it.

Next, I want you to describe your reason why. We talked about this, this is the motivation part, but I want you to make it matter. Describe the goal with the end in mind. Envision what your life could be like when you have accomplished this goal. Be as detailed as possible so your brain knows exactly what you will be working toward. Is it more free time with your family? Describe how it will feel to be with them and never miss another once in a lifetime event. Do you have the goal of buying a new car? Describe how it feels, sitting in the vehicle as you are surrounded by a luxurious interior. Is it your desired goal weight? Describe how you will feel when you are lighter and more capable of fitting into the clothes you want to wear. How about living an extraordinary relationship with the person you love. Describe the feeling you get when you are more affectionate and the words you speak to each other are kind and loving. Describe what you want as if you already know how it feels. Use your vivid imagination and describe your desire.

After you have described your life after your goal is accomplished, you need to declare that goal. Declare it to the other people in your life who matter to you. Tell those people why it is important to you. Tell those people that it matters because if you achieve this goal that you will feel like a better person. Will you be more available to them? Will you feel more confident? Will you be happier? Will you be healthier so that you live longer? Declare what you will do and why that matters to you.

As a side note on why declaring your goals is important, I want to make you aware of something. Besides the inner desire we have to reach certain levels of success in life, we have two other reasons that are part of what drives us to do what we do and don't do. We do things because we want to look good in front of other people. And we don't do things because we don't want to look bad in front of other people. We all have a desire to look good and a fear of looking bad. Some people have it at a much higher level than other people but everybody has it at some level. So if you declare your goals and declare what you are going to do to the people in your life who you want to look good in front of, well, guess what happens, that motivates you. You want to look good in front of those people, right? What happens if you declare those goals in front of someone you don't want to look bad in front of? That motivates you too, right. You don't want to look bad in front of that person, and you told them you were going to do something. Then when you declare it to them you say, "I want you to hold me accountable." I'm committed to achieving this goal, but it's a journey for me and I'm still working on my power of integrity. I'm still working on the skills that I'm learning and one of the skills is living my life by honoring my commitments. So could you please hold me accountable? Those people will do it for you if you want them to. When they ask you how you are going to reach your goals, then that is when the next D comes in.

The next step is to design a plan. You have to know exactly what you are going to do, when you are going to do it, and who is going to be involved, etcetera. You have to design a plan. You have to design a plan with all of the who, what, where, when, and why's that are going to be involved. How are you going to do it? Who is going to be involved? What's going to happen, where is it going to happen, when is it going to happen, and why is it going to happen. Design a plan in detail and those are going to be your steps. This is similar to what you learned in the ABC's of Success but it is much more psychological.

If you are accomplishing small goals, you don't need to design a detailed plan. If your goal is to clean the garage, do you really have to declare that to anybody? You can if you live with people and you are going to take some time away from your family and it's important for you to tell them. If it matters to you to clean the garage because it's weighing on your mind, then go ahead and declare that to the family. But if you live by yourself and your goal is to clean the garage on a Saturday afternoon, do you have to declare that to anybody? Not really. These goals and these D words aren't necessary for small goals. I didn't include this in The ABC's of Success because you are learning to see life at a higher level now. Why I want you to be a D student is because these are meant for your larger goals in life. So even if you do all of those previous Ds, if you are a perfect D student up to this point, unless you do the next thing, nothing happens. This next D was included in the ABC's of Success.

The next D is that you must do something. You must take action! Do something immediately. Get into momentum. Momentum is the key to blasting through the things that will stop you. Momentum is vital to overcoming the four blocks that we are going to talk about so that you can break through to the peak. When you are in momentum, it is really hard for things to stop you. So do something immediately and get into momentum right away. Don't wait for the 'time' to be right! I like to think of it this way. "If you wait for the time to be right, you may wind up with no time left." Take action now and create the time you need!

Our final D is to dedicate time. Dedicate time for yourself and don't let anyone or anything stand in your way. If you say, "I am going to do that, then do it." Decide, declare, do it when you said you were going to do it. That's integrity. Dedicate time for yourself and live with integrity.

So one more review. We will go over the D words and then I have to grade you. What are the D words again for achieving your goals at a higher level? Desire, no matter what goal you have, you have to have a desire. Then you need to get disgusted by the fact that you don't have that goal completed in your life yet. If you leave this earth before completing your desired goals then you would never leave it behind as your legacy. Next, you need to decide. Decide that now is the time. Say "I'm going to make a change right now. I've decided. Nobody's going to make me change my mind, I've decided, this is what I want for my life and I am going to get it!" Describe your reason why with the end result in mind. Make it matter to you. Make it matter to your life. Make it matter to the people in your life.

Then declare your goals to people who matter to you. Declare your goals to the people who you want to hold you accountable. Who do you not want to look bad in front of and who do you really want to look good in front of? Then design a plan. How are you going to do it, what's it going to take, who's going to be involved? Why are you going to do it, where are you going to do it? Design that plan. Then do something and get into momentum, immediately. Stay in momentum. Keep moving. Remember in order to put the smack down on what you want to achieve, you have to keep moving. If you keep moving, you stay in momentum. Finally dedicate time for yourself and don't let anyone or anything stand in your way. So if you can name all the Ds then I'm going to give you a D as your grade.

Congratulations, you are a perfect D student in achieving your goals!

Are you a 'D' student?

I have the **d**esire to

_____

_____

It **d**isgusts me that I am

_____

_____

I have **d**ecided to

_____

_____

I **d**escribe my reason as

_____

_____

I will **d**eclare this to

_____

_____

I have **d**esigned a plan to

_____

_____

I am going to **d**o this immediately

_____

_____

I will **d**edicate time for this goal

_____

_____

Emotions

The next area I want to cover are your emotions. Emotions are a very important part of your life to understand. They are a very important part of living the life that you want to live. Emotions can propel you forward or hold you back. So what are emotions?

I'm sure you know what they are, things like happy, sad, hurt, excited, giddy, scared, courageous, or any other feelings that you have given a name to, those are emotions. But, what are they? Emotions are feelings, right? We feel things like love. We can also feel paralyzing fear. We can feel anger, hate, rage, all of which I hope you don't feel very often. You can feel powerful, strong, useful and encouraged. These are emotions. There are hundreds of emotions that we know by name and we experience these emotions each day. Many times we use emotions to gauge how we feel. We often describe our life in terms of our feelings and emotions.

But what are emotions? What causes us to feel them? Our emotions are our thoughts combined with the story we are telling ourselves at the very moment that something happens and we give meaning to the event. Our thoughts are generated by the things that are happening around us at every moment of our lives. As humans, we have the desire to give meaning to those events.

Everything that happens around us at each moment of our lives produces a thought. But where the emotion actually comes from aren't the actual events, the words we hear, or even what we see, feel or experience. Emotions come from the meaning we give those thoughts, events and experiences and the story we create based on what we believe to be true. Emotions are based on our perception and our belief system. This is a very powerful lesson so make sure you are present and paying attention right now. I want you to think about nothing except what we are going over. If you are living somewhere else right now, if your thoughts are somewhere else, please start this lesson over again. If you need to take a break from reading, please do so now. I want to tell you exactly what I mean about the stories you tell yourself. This is the most important lesson of The Next Level.

I want to tell you a story. The purpose of this story is to help you understand how you allow your thoughts, perceptions, and emotions to affect your life. Here's what I want you to imagine. I want you to imagine that you got up an hour early to work on your goal like we talked about in the ABC's of Success. You've set your goal, you knew exactly what you needed to do, you took action, and you accomplished an important step in your goal that you planned to accomplish. You are having a great day. It's a beautiful, sunny day. You are feeling the emotion of extreme happiness because you are really living your life in a new way. You are proud of yourself and you can envision exactly what your life will be like when you accomplish this goal.

You're driving the typical route you take every day on your way to work. It's a normal day, nothing out of the ordinary is happening and as you approach a traffic light that you pass through every single day, you go to take a sip of your coffee. You don't need to stop for the light, because it just turned yellow. All of a sudden, out of nowhere, this jerk in a sports car cuts you off! You slam on your brakes and get stopped at the red light. You can't believe it, this guy almost hit your car, you spilled your coffee on yourself, and here he is taking off through the light that you were going to get through. What a jerk! You flip the guy off, call him a couple of names, and now you are really pissed off!

You went from being calm, happy and excited about your life to pissed off and angry in a matter of a moment because all of a sudden this guy, this inconsiderate jerk, cut you off! He probably doesn't even work, he's probably some trust fund baby coming off a three day party streak, and you can't believe this guy just cut you off like that. Why do people have to drive like that and where are the cops when this stuff happens? Why can't this guy get pulled over and learn his lesson. This is unbelievable. You're fuming mad, stopped at a red light with a new coffee stain on your shirt and this guy just ruined your day!

Can you see how that scenario might happen? Can you see how we can be living our lives and all of a sudden something happens which causes our emotions to instantly change how we feel? Something happens, then we look for the meaning behind it, and we make up a story. Is this guy really an inconsiderate jerk who is out to create a bad day for people? Does he get joy out of ruining people's lives because he was born into a wealthy family and gets a rush out of annoying people? Was he laughing at you as he saw you getting pissed off in his rear view mirror? What does it mean that he looked back at you and waved his hand?

Well, it doesn't mean anything. What happened doesn't mean that this guy is a jerk. It doesn't mean that he came from a wealthy family. It doesn't mean that he doesn't respect you. It doesn't mean he is a bad driver. It doesn't mean anything. You can give it any meaning that you want it to have. Let's look back on this event as it occurs again. We're not going to look through your filters, or through your belief system, or through your meaning, or through your perception. Let's look back at it from a camera that was positioned to see what happens at the intersection. If you were to watch this event back again you would see that you were approaching a traffic light. From behind you there was a car that was driving rather quickly. That car, in a rush to get through the light before it turned red, changed lanes very quickly and sped through the light. He kept going while you got stopped at the light. That's what happened. If you were viewing it from a camera that is what would have happened in this event.

Now in your car, you were taking a sip of your coffee at the very same moment that this car changed lanes and sped off in front of you. When that happened, you spilled your coffee on yourself because you got startled and slammed on your breaks. That's what happened. What you made it mean, and the story that you created was what caused you to feel the emotions you felt. Those emotions of anger, frustration, and rage didn't occur from the event. Did those emotions come from the fact that this guy changed lanes quickly and took off in front of you? No, that emotion, and that story came from the fact that you believed that this guy was an inconsiderate jerk who didn't care about you or anyone else for that matter, who changed lanes because he was just coming home from a three day party streak. That's the story. That's what you made up in your mind.

Now, I want to continue that story. That guy who was driving that car was not a trust fund baby. In fact that guy was one of the top brain surgeons in the entire area where you live. That guy was on his way to the hospital where your son was just air lifted by helicopter. Your son has a traumatic brain injury because on his way to school this morning, he got hit by a car. That guy, when he was just about your son's age lost his parents in a car accident. He made it his life's mission to be the best brain surgeon that he could ever be. He learned skills that no one else in the area has and he is the only surgeon in this area who can perform the type of surgery that your son needs to save his life. In his rush to get to the hospital to perform this brain surgery on your son, he did in fact speed. He did, in fact, see an opportunity to cut through traffic and make the light in his rush to get to the hospital to save the life of your son. That's what was happening in his car.

At the same moment that his car sped through that light, passing you, your phone rings and you see it's your spouse. You pick up the call and you start angrily telling them 'what happened'. "You won't believe what this guy just did. He cut me off in traffic just to make it through the light! I just spilled my coffee all over myself, you should see me, I'm a mess, and I'm so pissed right now!" Your spouse cuts you off and says, "Honey, I have some news, I have bad news. Our son was just hit by a car and he's being air lifted to the hospital right now. You hear that news and as you look up, you see the helicopter off in the distance. You forget all about what just happened to you. You slam on the gas, start speeding and cutting through traffic. In your rush to get to the hospital, you cut someone off as you change lanes quickly. That person spills their coffee on themselves when they slam on their brakes because of how you are driving. Now that person in that car yells at you, curses at you, thinks that you are a complete unorganized loser who can't get to work on time. They get pissed off at the fact that you've got to rush through traffic and cut people off just to get to work so that you won't get fired from your job. You're such an inconsiderate jerk!

As least that's the story that they tell themselves. Now is that really what's happening? No. That's a story. But through the camera, what would have happened. Your car would have sped up. You would have cut into another lane and took off. That's what happened through a lens with no filter of belief.

So do you see how these stories develop and how over time one story leads to another story and that story leads to another story. Now, if you just allowed your life to happen, simply experiencing life, emotions wouldn't run your life. I'm not saying whether it's right or wrong that this guy was cutting people off in traffic. However, I would have to say that if you were aware of what was going on in his life at that moment, you would have had a very different opinion of how this guy was driving. You would have said "Thank God I have the surgeon that has the ambition to get to the hospital to save the life of my son." You may have even prayed for his safety. You see our perception is what creates our stories. It's the meaning that you give to those perceptions, based on your belief, that creates those stories. You live within those stories and those stories cause an emotion.

We all make up some pretty wild stories based on our perception of what we think we know. We speculate about what we think is happening and we create a story about what happened, then we react based on our emotions. Many times we feel very strong emotions because of the story we tell ourselves. The story and the emotion have no basis in reality. They are a fabrication of the actual event that occurred. In order to learn how to control your emotions you need to learn to separate the story from what actually happened. You need to learn to tell the truth. The truth is only the truth if it can be proved from every perspective.

Our entire life is one big story told by us from our own point of view based on the events that occur at any given moment in time. The actual events have very little relation to our story. People don't have the ability to magically play back every event through the lens of a camera and say, "That's all that happened." They make up stories and live their lives in those stories from their own perspective and then feel emotions because of the story. That is a dangerous way to live. Please hear me and understand that I'm not saying you shouldn't have emotions. Emotion is an extraordinarily powerful driving force in our lives. In the Ds of goal setting, when I asked you to be a D student, one of the things I asked you to do was to get disgusted. That's an emotion. I wanted you to feel the emotion of being disgusted because you don't have what you want in your life.

You should, and I hope you do feel really strong emotions, when it's appropriate. You should feel love, and passion, and purpose and excitement. You should feel emotions at stronger levels than you have ever felt in your life, especially when you get done with this course. Our emotions shape our lives. Our thoughts create powerful emotions by creating feelings. Those feelings that we have, those emotions, they create the actions we take and those actions we take create our results.

Where most people run into a problem with their emotions is they allow their emotions to run their lives. They get so caught up in giving meaning to the events of their life and get stuck trying to make sense of what everything means. They get caught up in their emotions of frustration and anger and disappointment. They forget that life is about experiencing life at the moment it happens. There is what happens, and how we respond to what happens.

You experience emotion based on what you choose to feel. Many people have no idea about how we create our stories. You are always choosing to feel an emotion by deciding what you believe to be true. The more detailed the story, the more intense the emotion becomes. Most people are stuck in a story and their emotions drive their life. If people are stuck in the story that they are pissed off for some reason well then, what are they doing. They are living their life based on a story.

Are you getting this? I really hope so. Remember, our emotions are feelings we feel based on thoughts we have, based on the meaning we give events. We tell ourselves a story based on our own perceptions. Emotions are a complete fabrication of reality and they are one of the most powerful forces in our entire life. So how can you identify emotions and stop yourself from allowing negative emotions to run your life? I'm going to tell you but before I do, I want to give you a little warning. I want you to be careful when you are done with this section on emotions and stories. I want you to be very careful about starting to tell people how they are living in a story based on a feeling they have and an emotion they are creating based on the meaning they are trying to give their life. Don't start to say, "that's just a story," because most people don't understand it unless they've been taught properly how our thoughts aren't always the truth.

If you want the people in your life and the people in this world to start to understand all of this then they need to read this book too. Once people start to understand this information in the proper way, in the way that I teach it, from an unbiased opinion, they will get it. It's not the same coming from you who's telling them that they're living life in a story and the emotions they are feeling are just a complete fabrication of the events that occurred. That's not going to go too well if you try it that way. But imagine a world where people all thought at this level of understanding. I have imagined it and that is why I've created this book. So, please, don't start being a junior life coach and explaining to people how they are living in a story just because you have taken a five minute lesson on emotional understanding.

The big question still remains. Now that you know what emotions are, how can you use them to your advantage and live with emotion rather than allowing emotions to run your life? There are two ways to achieve this, and I'm going to teach you both.

The first thing we are going to do is focus on how to identify and quickly overcome negative emotions. Then I'm going to teach you to choose the emotion that you want to feel, and live in that emotion any time you want. Like everything else in life, there is a process. It is a matter of learning the steps, practicing, and enjoying the process of growing as a person. So let's take a look at the steps that it takes to control your emotions.

The first thing you need to do is recognize what negative emotion you are feeling. Are you feeling angry, jealous, sad, what is it? Not right now, obviously, because you might not be feeling any of those emotions, but the next time you are, the first thing you need to do to take control of your emotions is to recognize what emotion you are feeling in the moment. From now on, when you feel an emotion coming on, a really strong emotion, I want you to recognize that emotion. Give it a name and say "I am feeling _____"

Once you've given the emotion a name and identified it, you need to tell yourself why you are feeling this emotion. What did you see, hear or experience that started to stir up this emotion? It's important to recognize what is or what did occur. Tell the story (to yourself) in as much detail as you need to in order to give an explanation for the emotion.

Next, I want you to identify the story. This is different from telling the story. It is probably the most difficult thing for you to learn to do consciously. Your whole life you have been living in a story. During your lifetime, you have never stopped to identify the stories. You've just built story after story and built upon it and continued telling more stories and more stories one after the other. The stories you have told yourself up until now are the stories that have shaped your life. You tell stories because you think you know what's happening, based on what you allow yourself to believe and you give meaning to those events. When you are living in a story that is stirring a negative emotion, you are living in a negative disbelief.

Identifying the story requires you to think outside of your own beliefs. A great question to ask yourself is "Is this true?" Unless you know, because you have evidence to prove it's true, from every perspective, then it's nothing more than a belief. Beliefs are nothing more than a story. In fact, even if there is proof and you believe something to be true, isn't it possible that someone or something can prove otherwise in the future? We choose what we believe. If you choose a negative disbelief, you will have a negative emotion. Negative disbeliefs come from not thinking realistically. What I am saying can be clarified by this question. "Isn't it possible that the story you are telling yourself is not true?" In order for you to answer that question with a "No," you would have to be close minded. In the ABC's of Success, you learned that you need to be open minded to succeed.

The next step in controlling your emotions is to tell the truth. What actually happened? This is another really difficult thing for people to do. At this point you have to choose to be honest with yourself. You must identify the truth and accept it as what happened. Look at the event and break it down, what actually happened? You must completely eliminate any story about what happened that made you feel the emotion. You eliminate your story by allowing something else to be possible. Again, the question is "Isn't it possible that the story you are telling yourself is not true?"

Once you have eliminated the story, once you tell the truth of what actually happened, you need to do the next really difficult thing. You have to acknowledge your role in the events that occurred. Are you really ready to make a massive difference in your life and in the life of the people around you? This is the biggest step. When you can learn to do this along with the other steps in controlling your emotions, it is incredibly powerful. You must acknowledge your role in the event that just happened. You don't need to accept responsibility for the entire event, just your role. What did you do or not do during this event? Don't make yourself right or wrong. Don't make anyone else right or wrong. Just acknowledge your role. Acknowledge specifically what you did. What actually happened? What did you do?

This becomes easier as you begin practicing a valuable lesson in life. The lesson is learning about right and wrong. When you spend your life making people right and wrong, you spend your life in a story. My advice to you is to stop making people right and wrong, including yourself. There is what happened, our belief system, and a new moment in time. If you view something as right, it's because you believe it. If you view something as wrong, it's because it's not in line with your beliefs. There is no actual right and wrong. There is only what you believe. You can adjust the question to say the same thing by saying "Isn't it possible that what you believe is not true?"

Let's get back to our steps in controlling your emotions. Don't make people right, don't make people wrong. Don't make yourself right, don't make yourself wrong. Just tell the truth. What happened? Acknowledge your role and your responsibility in the event. After you acknowledge your role, you need to accept it. You have to accept the fact that the event just happened or maybe that event is still happening. You must fully, completely, and whole heartedly accept it as what already happened or what is happening. Is there anything you can do about what already happened in your life? Is there anything you can do to change your past? Is there anything that you can do to alter the events that already occurred in your life? No. So why would you spend even one second, one moment, one millisecond living in an emotion from an event that occurred in the past.

If the event is over, is that event happening in your life right now? No. What caused you to feel the emotion already happened and you are choosing at this moment to stay in that negative emotion. In order to get angry, jealous, or any other negative emotion that involves you and someone else, you would have to believe that they were wrong. You would have to start making that person wrong. What meaning are you giving to the event that occurred? When you stop giving meaning to the events and when you stop making people wrong all the time, you will stop feeling negative emotions. I'm not saying that they were right in what they did. I'm just saying that you need to stop making them responsible for how you feel based on the events that occur in your life. Most people live their lives stuck because they are feeling emotions they felt based on a story that already occurred in their past and they can do nothing about it. But somehow they live their lives around these events.

People do this with events that they label as good and bad. They keep living the event over and over and over again. They are living in the past instead of living in the present moment. But those emotions, those stories, they are nothing more than memories of event's which have already occurred but no longer exist. They have no bearing on the future and they have no bearing on the present. They are your past and you are choosing to live in your past. A lot of people love to live those emotions over and over and over again. That is their choice. Let me ask you a question. Can you drive a car by only looking in the rearview mirror? Of course not. Maybe you could for a short time. But if you spend too much time focusing on what is behind you, you are going to destroy what is in front of you. So stop looking in the rearview mirror of your life and focus on really living in the moment and paying attention to what's happening now, what's right there in front of you. Stop telling stories, forgive people quickly and choose to believe instead that what occurred was nothing more than a test in your emotional control.

Finally, after you have done all of that, you have to choose what emotion you want to feel and live that emotion in this new moment. Take a deep breath. Consciously change your emotion. You are living now. Your past has already occurred. It is your past. If what you have right now is a negative emotion, what would you have to be doing in this moment in order to have that negative emotion in your life? You would have to be living in your past. You would have to be living in a story. You would have to be making someone wrong.

Now what would you have to do in order to have a positive emotion in your life? You would have to be living in the present moment. You would have to be okay with what happens in your life at all times. You would have to be accepting. You would have to be aware that your life is nothing more than what is happening right now. In order to have a positive emotion in your life, you would have to be doing what? You would have to be choosing a positive emotion in your life at this present moment. Now isn't that a revelation. Yes, you can choose to feel happy at any time, no matter what. You can choose to feel motivated at any time. You can choose to feel loving at any time. You can also choose to feel pissed off. You can choose to feel angry. You can choose to feel frustrated. But that is your choice.

The way to control your emotions is to follow the steps that I outlined. Identify the emotion, recognize the story, tell the truth and so on. As you are learning to control your negative emotions so they don't control you, it's likely you will need to follow this process closely. The really good news is that in reality, you can eliminate every step and just be in emotion. Emotions are nothing more than a choice. You choose how you feel at every moment of your life. I'm going to give you a simple, fill in the blank sentence to illustrate what I mean.

Fill in the blank

I want you to practice this statement. It goes like this: <u>Blank</u> I am choosing to <u>blank</u>.

What this sentence allows you to do is to take anything that is happening in your life and identify it. The first <u>blank</u> is 'what is happening.' So 'blank (what)' is happening. Fill in the blank with what is happening in your life.

The next part of the sentence is "I am choosing to 'blank'." After 'what is happening' comes your choice. So if you are choosing to be pissed off, then that is your choice. If you are choosing to yell, that's your choice.

The next sentence reads, "I <u>blank</u> so <u>blank</u>." The first blank is the action you chose to take, followed by "So blank." That is your result.

Let's fill in the whole thing together. 'Blank' I am choosing to 'blank'. I 'blank' so 'blank'. Sounds kind of funny, right? The way that this works is you will say, "what is happening?" So perhaps you say, "A car is cutting me off in traffic." That's what's happening. "I am choosing to (be or do what.)" Are you choosing to be understanding that maybe this person has something going on where they are forced to get somewhere really quickly or are you choosing to make it mean that they are a jerk and an inconsiderate loser? What are you making it mean? You could say, "Some guy is cutting me off in traffic, I am choosing to allow it to happen and not get upset." You are allowed to have that action, it's your choice. You can be or do anything you choose.

In the next blank you can fill in, "I am allowing this to happen" so I 'what' is your result? Well, you could fill in the blanks like this. "Some guy is cutting me off in traffic and I am choosing to get pissed off, blow my horn and flip him off. I am choosing to get pissed off, blow my horn and flip him off, so I am in an angry state and having road rage."

Do you see how this works? What is happening? What are you choosing to be or do because of it? That choice is going to create your result for the present moment of your life. I'm hoping that this example is helping me to illustrate to you how we can make up these stories in our lives and how we choose to respond. I hope that you are aware of the fact that you will continue to make up these stories. However, I want you to be more aware of it when it's happening so you can begin to live realistically, in the present moments of your life.

I want this example to remind you of how you make up stories. I used this example to make this lesson easy to remember. Just remember the word car, C A R. I want you to remember that your life is caused by your C A R. You have a Choice in how you respond to what happens to you. The choice that you make will cause you to take an Action. And the action that you take will cause you to have a Result. Choice, Action, Result. C A R. Remember the car story when you are faced with the question of whether or not you are living in a story. Say, "Wait a second. I am making a choice as to how I am going to be or what I am going to do in this moment. In this moment, what I choose to be or do is going to cause me to take a certain action and that action is going to have a result. What result do I want to have?"

Learn to ask and answer this question first, "What result do I want to have?" When you decide first what result you want to have, then you are in full control of your emotions. If you choose that no matter what happens to you, your result is that you will be happy, then you already know the result. In order for you to be happy all the time, you would have to know that you would accept everything that happens to you. The action you would have to take at all times is to smile, forgive, and allow life to just happen instead of making up a story. Can you imagine being so in control of your emotions at all times that you could choose what emotion you want to feel at every moment, every second, and every day of your life? No matter what happens to you, you control your emotions. Can you imagine that? I have and that is one of the reasons I needed to write this book.

Is being in complete control of your emotions at all times possible for you? I think by now, you realize that anything is possible. But is it realistic to always be 100% in control of your emotions at every moment of your life? It's possible, it's just not realistically going to happen. It will however become much easier for you, the more you practice. Make the choice of how you want to be in your life, the moment you wake up in the morning. Consciously be aware of your emotions and continue to be aware throughout the day, so when things happen to you, you don't have to make up a story. You don't have to make every event mean something. You can choose to be what you want to be in your life. You can choose to be happy no matter what happens to you. That is a powerful way to live.

This focus on emotions is probably the most intense and thought provoking area that you have read so far. I want to encourage you to read it again. When you can grasp and embrace what you just learned with an open heart and an open mind, your life will make a drastic shift. This lesson is something that very few people will ever grasp in life. If you are one of the few, look out! You are going to be one of the rare people in life who take 100% responsibility for your own life. When you do this, you will be challenged in a way you've never experienced before. I invite you to take that challenge. Take responsibility for everything that happens in your life but don't make yourself wrong or right. Allow life to happen. When you find yourself in a negative emotion based on a negative disbelief, choose to forgive as quickly as possible. This will get you out of your story and bring you back to the present moment where you can fully live your life.

Making blank promises

Anticipate some things that might happen to you. Here is an example. <u>When someone tailgates my vehicle</u> I am choosing to <u>let them pass me and not get angry.</u> I <u>let them pass me</u> so <u>I was able to stay calm and get them out of my life.</u>

I am choosing

to_____

I_____

So

_____.

I am choosing

to_____

I_____

So

_____.

I am choosing

to_____

I_____

So

_____.

The Rules of the Blame Game

Before we go on I want to introduce you to a game that will help you identify when people, including you, are living in a story. This game is played every day by people and it is going to be very clear to you after this lesson, who plays this game the most. You have probably heard it before, I'm sure you have probably even played it most of your life. The name of the game is the blame game. It is played by two or more people, suitable for all ages, and most people play it their entire life. It's the game that is played when people fail to acknowledge their role in their own lives. I don't know if anyone has ever written the rules of this game before so I went ahead and wrote the rules to this game so people know how to actually play it.

So here are the rules to the blame game. It is always played by at least two people. The person who plays the game the most always loses. If you think your emotions are caused by other people, you lose. If you blame other people for the way you feel, you lose. If you go through life blaming other people for what happens to you, you lose. So you lose the game by thinking that your emotions are caused by other people, blaming other people for how you feel, and by blaming other people for what happens to you. That's how you lose the blame game.

Now, how do you win the blame game? The only way to win the blame game is to realize that the other people who are playing the game don't actually have to know that they are playing. If you can successfully blame other people for the way your life goes, how you feel, and for your emotions, without them even knowing it, then you can win every single time at the blame game.

Remember the rules though; the one who plays the game the most, always loses. This rule is the most important rule because at the same time the blame game is going on, there is another game going on. That game is the game of life. It's your life, it's happening at the same time. Life is also a game and you can play it at whatever level you want. Simultaneously, any time you are playing the blame game, the game of life is always happening as well. Those who choose to play the blame game lose at the game of life. Those who choose to play the game of life always lose the blame game.

I don't know about you but I choose not to play the blame game. I choose to play the game of life and I choose to have a lot of fun at it. I would rather allow the losers who think they are the winners at life to play the blame game and to think that they are winning. Because they are winning the blame game if they are blaming other people for their lives. For me though, I don't care if I lose the blame game because I don't even want to play it. I want to win at the game of life. If you want to win at the game of life, then you need to stop playing the blame game. Right now, if you don't ever want to play the blame game again just choose to quit. Just say, "I'm done playing the blame game" and don't ever play it again.

Exercise in emotional control

I would like to do an exercise in controlling your emotions. This exercise typically helps people who don't understand how emotions are a story and how they create that story based on what meaning they give life. This exercise is a very powerful one and I want to encourage you to do it when you are in a quiet place and you can really focus. I want you to be able to experience these emotions on a very intense level. I want you to really live in the moment as though it were occurring. This exercise is going to be occurring in the moment but what I am going to ask you to do is return to a time in your past when you felt a really strong emotion. This can get intense for some people. If you are not able to do this exercise right now, then I'm going to ask you to skip this section and go back to it when you are actually able to do it.

If you are able to do this exercise I think you are going to find it very beneficial in recognizing how you can, in fact, control your emotions. I'm going to lay out this exercise differently because it's meant to be experienced, not just read. I would like you to be alone when you do this exercise. Sit in a nice comfortable location and relax. I'm going to ask you a series of questions. Don't write the answers down, just experience the event like you did the first time it was happening. Allow yourself to really let go and feel. This exercise should take you about 10 minutes. Read each line and do what it says or answer the question. Just be in your mind.

Let's begin:

Think of a time in your life when you felt a really strong negative emotion. What was it? What was the emotion?

Where were you?

What was the environment like?

What was the weather?

Really get into that moment in your life. How did you feel?

Were you feeling tense? Were you clenching your fists?

Were you clenching your jaw? Were your muscles tight?

How did your body feel? Did you feel heavy and unable to move freely?

What was being said to you at that time or what was happening?

What were you saying to yourself?

How did the people around you appear? Did they appear against you?

I want you to recognize that emotion very deeply and completely.

Really get into that emotion.

Feel it more.

More.

Allow yourself to really feel that emotion.

You might find yourself shaking, clenching your jaw and your fists. You might feel like you are ready to cry.

Whatever that emotion is I want you to feel it. Feel it in your heart. Feel it in your stomach.

Now what made you feel this emotion?
What is the story you were telling yourself?

What are you making the events that are happening mean?

If someone is saying something to you, what are you making it mean?

If something is happening to you. What are you making it mean?

What is the story?

Now, I want you to look at the event as if a camera had viewed and filmed the entire event.

What actually happened at that moment?

What happened in the moments leading up to the event?

Tell the truth. Look at what happened.

Look at what you did.

Look at what the other person did.

See what is going on.

Tell the truth. What happened?

Now, acknowledge your role in the event.

What did you do or not do in the moment and in the few moments leading up to the event?

Once you have acknowledged your role, fully and completely, you need to eliminate any blame. You need to stop blaming the other person for what happened. They played a role, absolutely, but so did you. In order for you to feel a negative emotion, you would have to believe that they were responsible for what happened. That is playing the blame game.

I need you to choose not to blame.

Now, accept the event.

Accept it. It happened.

There is nothing that you can do about it.

The event already occurred. It is your past.
I want you to choose what emotion you want to feel.

What positive emotion do you want to feel?

Do you want to feel happy?

Do you want to feel love?

Do you want to feel acceptance?

Do you want to feel appreciation?

What positive emotion will you choose to feel, now?

If you are feeling happy then what would you do in order to have the emotion of happy?

You would smile.

If you choose to feel the emotion of love then you would open your heart.

If you choose to feel the emotion of acceptance, then you will open your arms.

You get to choose the emotion that you want to feel.

Feel that emotion.

Recognize that emotion.

Really feel that emotion.

Are you smiling?

Identify what made you feel this emotion.

If you are having a problem identifying it, I will tell you. It was a choice.

You chose to feel this emotion, the same way you chose to feel the negative emotion.

Continue to feel that emotion.

Continue to smile.

Laugh if you want to.

Go deeper into that positive emotion and live there as if that is the only emotion in the world right now.

No matter what is going on in the world around you right now, you choose to feel this positive emotion.

Focus on that emotion, feel it, let it go.

Is your body feeling lighter as if you can move more freely and openly? As if it is the greatest feeling on earth.

You have never felt this free before!

It's the best feeling you could ever imagine!

You always want to feel this way!

Feel it!

Live it!

Be in this moment!

As you are living that emotion I want you to understand something important.

You are choosing to feel that emotion right now and you can choose to feel this positive emotion any time. Continue to feel it.

Live it.

Be that emotion......

END

As we end this exercise I want you to continue to feel that emotion. I want you to go and live that emotion in your life. I want you to know that no matter what happens in your life, you are in control of your emotions and how you feel. You choose what emotions that you feel at every single moment of your life.

Think of life as a movie that you write, direct and star in every day. You write the script of your life. If the character you want to play is always happy then live and be that character. You can influence other people to live in better, positive, more open, happy, loving, giving and caring emotions by being that yourself. Being able to control your emotions is so powerful. It is such a drastic influence on other people's lives. You can influence and affect the world around you by how you are choosing to be and what emotions you are <u>choosing</u> to feel at every moment of every day. Practice it. Live in that emotion. You now know how to get yourself into a positive emotion at any time. You choose to. So choose to be happy and choose to be funny, and choose to be silly, choose to be giving, and choose to be loving, and choose to be caring and choose to be open. Choose your emotions and live that in your life.

What has been stopping you?
Complete these sentences and then read them as affirmations daily.

Emotions – One of the 4 things that stop us in life!

I recognize that my negative emotions are nothing more than a story and I'm not going to allow

_____

to control how I feel or live my life any more.

I recognize that my negative emotions are nothing more than a story and I'm not going to allow

_____

to control how I feel or live my life any more.

I recognize that my negative emotions are nothing more than a story and I'm not going to allow

_____

to control how I feel or live my life any more.

I recognize that my negative emotions are nothing more than a story and I'm not going to allow

_____

to control how I feel or live my life any more.

Influence

The next area we are going to cover is a huge area. It is so huge it is all around you, you can't get away from it. It's everywhere, it's everything. If you look around you right now, it's all around you. So what are we going to talk about?

We are going to talk about the influence in your life. What is influencing you right now? What are you allowing to influence you in your everyday life? Influence is everywhere. It's huge. It's all around us and it's inescapable.

Influence is power. Influence is pressure. Influence is what makes you sway in a certain direction. Influence is authority and control. Influence can manipulate you and persuade you into doing things. Influence is able to talk you into and out of doing things. Influence is that thing that can win you over. Influence has the ability to affect our lives. Influence has the ability to inspire us or destroy us. Influence is able to encourage us, stimulate us and hold us down. Influence is everything, everywhere and everyone.

So that's what we are going to talk about right now. That tiny little thing called influence. Wait a minute. Didn't I just say that influence was huge, all around us, everybody and everything? Didn't I say that influence was everywhere and that you can't get away from it? Didn't I say that? So how can I say that influence is a teeny, tiny, little thing? I'm going tell you, but not quite yet.

Influence has been affecting you from the moment you were born. Influence is everything. Influence is the air you breathe, the food you eat, the music you listen to, the television shows that you watch. It's your family, it's your friends. Influence can control your thoughts, control your emotions, control the way you think, control the way you dress and the decisions you make. Influence can literally control everything that you have in your life. Influence is everywhere. So how can I possibly say that influence is such a little thing?

I say that because I know who you are. I know who you are as a human being. You, my friend, are bigger than influence. You are bigger than any influence around you, if you choose to be. If influence is everything and you are bigger than it, then you in essence are the biggest and most powerful force in your life.

You are influence! You are power! You are control! You sway the direction that you want to go. You apply the weight and pressure that's needed to guide your life. You persuade yourself, manipulate yourself, induce yourself, talk yourself into and out of anything. You affect your life. You have the ultimate affect on your life. You shape it and you create it. So if you have that kind of power and if you are bigger than the influences around you, then influence becomes a really small thing, if you choose to be bigger than it.

Right now I want you to focus on the first word that I used about influence. The first word I used was power. Influence is power and if you are influence then you are power. Have you ever considered how powerful you are? Have you ever really wondered what you are capable of achieving? For many years I hadn't either. I viewed myself smaller than I know I am. How did this happen?

Remember in my story, I was doing everything from the vantage point of the outside in. I was creating my life from the outside in. I was allowing the outside influences of my life to be bigger than me. So I just forgot that I was the most powerful influence in my life. Perhaps you have forgotten that too.

I forgot that I was bigger than the influences around me. I forgot that I had the ultimate power. I forgot that my life was mine to live. I forgot that I have a purpose and just living my life by going to work every day and doing the day in and day out routine of my life, wasn't who I am as a human being. I forgot that all of those things around me, including my children, were influences.

Then I realized that I am bigger than those influences, yes, I'm bigger than my children, but what I'm saying is that as an influence your children can either influence you or you can influence them. You'll see what I mean when I am through with this chapter on influence. I realized again that I get to choose what I allow into my life and what I choose to keep out of my life. I began to allow myself to be the biggest influence in my life. I gave myself back the power to live and control my life. When I began to fight back the negative influences and assert my power and my influence over my life, everything started to change.

That's what I want for you. I want you to realize that you are bigger than any influences that you'll face in your life. We talked about associations but associations are different than influences. Associations are who and what are around you. Influences are what's around you and how it affects your life if you let it. What negative outside associations are you allowing in your life and while you are allowing them into your life what influences are they asserting over you? Those influences do a really good job, if you let them, of eating up your energy and your time.

Much like associations, there are two different types of influences. There are personal influences, much like there were personal associations. There are also outside influences just like there are outside associations, such as the non living things and the places that you go. The outside influences are the things that are in your life for which you really don't have to consider their feelings. You don't have to consider emotion when you are dealing with outside influences. You aren't going to hurt the feelings of the can of soda, or the tv, or any other outside influence. However, could you hurt the feelings of the personal influences in your life? Absolutely. Especially if they don't understand how to control their emotions like you do.

Regardless of the influence in your life, regardless of whether it is personal or an outside influence, unless you begin to influence yourself to make the changes in your life, you are going to get stuck behind those influences and those influences are going to hold you down. Those personal influences are those people around you who place pressure on you to do certain things. They hold you down from reaching the peak in your life. They might say, "No, don't do that because it's not possible." Those people press influence on you and they try to hold you down. They try to block you from getting to where you want to go.

It is kind of like peer pressure for adults. Peer pressure is huge for adults because we make our own choices more easily. As children we are effected by peer pressure but we can't make as many of our own choices quite as easily. Children are kind of governed by their parents and what their parents allow them to do. But as adults you get to choose everything.

So who are your personal influences? They are your parents, your spouse, your children, your siblings, your friends, your neighbors, your co-workers, restaurant workers, retail workers and any other person, any other human being that you come in contact with. Any other person is a personal influence and a personal association at some level. This also includes the people that you have contact with online in social media. The friends that you have can influence you if you allow them to. Personal influences are all around us every day.

You can only do one thing at a time when it comes to influence. You can either be influenced by the personal or outside influences around you or you can be influencing the people around you. You can't do both at the same time. Sure, there are times when you can go from influencing someone to being influenced in a very short amount of time but you can't do both simultaneously. The people around you are constantly, unknowingly, attempting to influence you out of achieving your goals and living the life that you want to live. In order to be aware of how influence works, I want you to begin to view life and make decisions based on a well thought out, fully understood, multi directional perspective of life. Does that sound complicated? Well, it's not but it does take some practice and it's going to take me teaching you how to do it and in order for me to do that effectively, I want to paint a picture for you of how influence happens at various times throughout our life. We're going to go back to the goal of losing twenty pounds.

A Story of Influence

So you have set a goal of losing twenty pounds. You have declared that goal to the people in your life. You declared it to the people that you usually go to happy hour with from work. You want them to hold you accountable. You clarified your expectation to them that you want to achieve your goal of losing twenty pounds and because of that you have asked them not to invite you to happy hour. When you were declaring your goal of losing twenty pounds to the people at work, you influenced a co-worker to hit the gym with you.

Your co-worker is excited, because she has been looking for a leader and you have just influenced her. She was kind of tired of going out to happy hour after work and she set a goal of losing twenty pounds too. You are working together and motivating each other to make that happen. The two of you form a plan of going to the gym every day after work instead of going to happy hour. Your plan consists of leaving immediately after work together and you are going to do this Monday thru Friday. So Monday you get to the gym. Tuesday you go to the gym. Wednesday and Thursday you get to the gym. Friday rolls around and everybody in the office had a really rough day.

It was really stressful, lots of things happened, and you are tired. You are really not feeling like going to the gym. Nonetheless, you think, "you know what, I'm going to live with integrity, I'm going to live with commitment and I promised my co-worker that I would go to the gym, so I'm going to go." As you are getting ready to pack up your desk, another co-worker comes over and she says, "Hey, we missed having you at happy hour this week, it's just not the same without you. I know you've been working on your goal, but what do you say, just for tonight, you come out with us? Come on it's Friday night! Aren't you ready to just be done with today? We all had a horrible, rough day, and we're all stressed out. What do you say you skip the gym, go to the bar with us and have a few drinks?"

Wow, that's a tough influence right there. Here you are already having a battle in your head about whether or not you want to go to the gym because you are tired, and there you are faced with an influence. You are really kind of caught because there is part of you that says, "I don't really want to go to the gym" and then there is another part of you that says, "I do want to go to the gym because I made this commitment and I promised myself that I would go to the gym."

But you say, "You know what, I am tired today. I'm stressed out. I'm going to go to happy hour with you." So, you pack up your things and you go over to your co-worker's desk and you say "Hey listen, I think it's awesome that we've been hitting the gym every day. I just found out everyone else is going to that new place down the street. I know we said we would hit the gym, but just for tonight, I was thinking that maybe you and I should join them and then we can get back on track on Monday. What do you say?"

Your co-worker reluctantly says "Okay, alright, that's fine and we'll get back on track on Monday." They pack up their things and off the two of you go and you hit the bar for happy hour with the rest of the people.

Let's look at this from a well thought out, fully understood, multi-directional perspective of life. What does it say from your perspective? Are you honoring your commitment to yourself? Are you living with integrity? I understand that you have the choice of whether or not to go to the bar or go to the gym. It's your choice. You know that whatever action you choose to take, you live with that result. But what does it say about how you are committed to living? Are you committed to living a life of integrity and of commitment? You're saying yes to others, and you are saying no to yourself. You are allowing yourself to be smaller than the influence.

What does it say to your co-worker who also committed to going to the gym? Does it say that you are committed to her and to helping her achieve her goals as well? No, it doesn't. You are showing her that she is still being influenced by you. Of course she can make up her own mind, she can make her own decisions and her own choices and could have said, "You know what, you go ahead and go to the bar, I'm going to go hit the gym." However, since she is still living in your influence, she makes the choice to go with you instead.

Now, what does it say from the perspective of your other co-workers? Don't your actions say "I'm not really committed, I'm interested in losing this weight, but you can talk me out of it? Even though I asked you to not invite me and even though I asked for you to honor that request, I'm going to let it go. I'm not going to require that you live up to my expectations and I'm going to go ahead and hit the bar with you tonight."

You were faced with a decision. You decided between bar and gym. Then you made the choice to go to the bar instead. You went to your coworker's desk and you influenced her to go with you. She made a decision to go to the bar with you. You went to the bar. You had food, you had drinks, you went home, you woke up with a headache and you are pissed off, disappointed, feeling guilty or some other negative emotion because you made a choice that wasn't in line with who you want to be. Who knew the power of one choice, based on one influence?

Influences – Another of the things that can stop you

I recognize that

_____

is a negative influence in my life and I am no longer going to allow that to stop me from achieving my goals.

I recognize that

_____

is a negative influence in my life and I am no longer going to allow that to stop me from achieving my goals.

I recognize that

_____

is a negative influence in my life and I am no longer going to allow that to stop me from achieving my goals.

What Does It Mean

So, think about the story, what meaning are you giving the events that occurred? Are you making it mean that you are a failure? Are you making it mean that you can't honor your commitments? Are you making it mean that you can't live a life of integrity? Are you making your co-worker wrong because she came up to your desk and invited you when you clearly told everyone that you didn't even want to be invited? What are you making it mean that is allowing you to feel pissed off, disappointed or guilty right now? Well, that's the story.

The story part is what you make the events of your life mean. If you make your choice mean all of those things, then you created a story around that event. So identify the story that you are telling yourself. Obviously this is a fictional story but I'm sure that you will be able to put yourself in a similar situation where you have been influenced in your life. If you can do that for yourself right now, I want you to tell the truth. What actually happened? Well in this example, you would have to say. "Alright, here is what happened. I was feeling stressed and stress is an emotion. I must have been feeling stress because I made up a story about what I made the day mean. Because I was feeling stressed I allowed the influence that was put upon me to make a choice to go to the bar. I chose to go to the bar."

In order to continue with what we learned previously, you would have to acknowledge your role in the event. What happened? You said "yes, I will go to the bar." You influenced your friend to go to the bar with you. You went to the bar and you went home. That's what happened. Acknowledge your role. Can you do anything about what already happened? No.

Now just accept it. You're not wrong for doing what you did. You simply made a choice that was not in line with your belief about what you want for your life. Just accept it. No one is wrong in this situation. There is what happened, and then there is the story.

Finally, I want you to choose what emotion you would be feeling at this time. Instead of feeling pissed off, angry and disappointed in yourself and making up the story that you aren't able to honor your commitments and live with integrity, choose to feel an emotion that is positive instead. Choose to have a feeling of appreciation that you have such wonderful friends that care about you and who want to be around you. Choose to feel the emotion that you are happy to be alive. Sure, you messed up, but we can fix that. Choose what emotion you want to feel and live in that emotion.

Now, how could you re-live that entire event back and make a better choice? Well, here is how you do it and here is how you view your life from that multi directional perspective. The first thing you need to do is be aware of influence. You need to be aware that your co-workers invitation is an influence. It was a harmless invitation. All she was doing was inviting you to go out. However, if you are faced with a choice, you are either being influenced, or you are influencing.

Second, don't allow yourself to be smaller than the influence. If you are allowing your co-worker to influence you to go to the bar, who is bigger? The influence is bigger. Who is smaller? You are. Now if you want to be bigger than every influence around you, then you would not allow those influences to be bigger than you at that moment. So don't do that. Don't allow those influences to be bigger than you.

Third, you need to honor your commitments to yourself and to others. You need to do what you said you would do long after the mood that you said it in has disappeared. You didn't feel like going to the gym today but you said that you would hit the gym every single day, Monday through Friday, and you promised that to someone else as well. If you go to the bar, you didn't honor your commitment to yourself or to her. So you would have to make the choice to be an influence. You would need to be an influence in your decision making. When you make the positive choice of what to do and that choice affects the life of another, that makes you a leader. You would have to make a choice to be a leader who influences others in a positive way or to be influenced by others and allow them to lead your life.

As a leader, you need to be willing to stand up for what you believe, despite possible ridicule. So in this situation when you were invited to happy hour you could have said, "No, I don't think so, not tonight. Thanks for the invitation but we're going to the gym." Your co-worker could go back to the rest of the people who are getting ready to go to the bar and say, "You wouldn't believe what just happened. I invited them to go to the bar with us and they just blew me off. I bet they go to the gym and talk about us behind our backs because they think they're better than us for going to the gym…."

Wow, what a story. Is any of that true? You were invited and respectfully declined the invitation. That's what happened. What happens when people make up stories? Typically, tension arises and instead of talking about what is causing the tension, it drives a wedge in between the relationship. This can happen with any relationship. If you make up stories because you give something meaning, tension will arise in your life.

Now that you have new knowledge, you can answer from a multi directional perspective. You understand that most people live within a story. In order to counteract this tendency in others, you have to really think about how you are going to speak to people from now on in order to be an influence.

You could now respond to the invitation by saying, "You know, I really appreciate the invitation. Thank you for thinking of me. Believe me; it's not that I don't want to go with you, because there is a huge part of me that does. I have to tell you that this extra weight I'm working on losing is really bothering me. I've got to lose this weight. It's been bothering me for a really long time. It's been great to have a partner in this journey because it helps keep me motivated. The two of us together are keeping each other on track. When I reach my goal I plan on celebrating it, so I'll join you then because I do miss you too. I really appreciate you thinking of me and wanting to hang out and if you want to go to the gym with me at any point and grab a healthy dinner afterwards I'm all for it. But I'm going to skip happy hour today and I hope you can understand my reason."

Do you think that they might understand that and do you think that you might have answered it from a multi directional perspective? I think you have. That takes some practice and it takes some courage and it takes honesty and openness and commitment and all of those things that you have to choose to be in your life. And yes, it takes energy. It takes energy to stand up for yourself. It takes energy to stand there and fight back influence, it really does. But the more you do it and the more consistent you are, the better you will get at it. Now, what does that say about you? How does that look from a multi directional perspective? Have you just told yourself that you are bigger than the influences around you? Have you just told yourself that you can live a life of integrity and commitment and honor what you say you are going to do? Absolutely it does. Congratulations for that.

So how about from the perspective of the friend who has been joining you? Doesn't it say from their perspective that you do honor your commitments, that you live a life of integrity, she is important to you, she matters and that you are there for her? Doesn't it reinforce that you are going to be a positive influence in her life? Absolutely it does. You are being a leader at that point.

What about from the perspective of your other co-workers? From their perspective it says, "Wow, they really are committed to their goal and I get it. They honor our friendship and just because they aren't hanging out with us every night doesn't mean that we aren't friends. They are really working on their goal right now and I respect that. In fact, I kind of want some of that in my life too….."

So while you are learning to make decisions and make choices and do all that from the multi directional point of view, you need to start asking yourself some questions. Again, the more you practice this stuff, the easier it will get and it will all become automatic.

When you want to be an influence, learn to ask yourself these questions.

"Am I honoring my commitment to myself and others and living a life of integrity for myself and others?"

"Am I speaking from the understanding that people may make up a story if I'm not perfectly clear in my intentions."

Being an influence is being a leader. I encourage you to be a leader in your life! Practice these leadership skills in your daily life. Recognize influence and know that you are bigger than any personal or outside influence.

Ask yourself, "Will this choice move me closer to or further away from where I want to be?"

Look at the decision you will make and consider how it will affect you and others.

Be courageous enough to say no to the influence and in turn say yes to yourself.

Be clear in your communications to others.

Leaders know that power is achieved through influence. Leadership is influence! Remember, if you are standing alone, you only have the power of yourself. When you develop the power of influence and you can influence others to join you, then you have the power of all of those who you have influenced to join you. So if you are looking to influence the world in a big way, then you have to start by yourself and then influence one person to join you. Then you influence another, and another.

The way to build tremendous influence in this world is to teach people how to influence others to join your cause. When you teach people how to influence and as their influence grows, your ability to affect this world in a big way grows exponentially. So at first, you must stand alone. Once you have grown to the point where you are able to influence others, that is when you will start to see amazing growth and amazing change in your life.

Humans Make Mistakes

I want to do a quick check before we move forward. Are you human? If you answered 'yes" then we can keep going but if you answered "no" you can skip this entire section. This entire section is actually for humans. This section is about setbacks and if you are human you are probably going to experience setbacks in your life. You are probably going to fail, you are probably going to fall down, and you are probably going to make mistakes. So if you're not human, go ahead and skip this section but if you are human then we should probably cover all this. Knowing how to deal with setbacks is one of the most important aspects of living your life powerfully, living your life at your peak and achieving your goals. Humans make mistakes. Humans fail, they fall out of integrity and they don't honor their commitments from time to time. It's natural. It's not impossible to live a life of complete integrity, complete commitment one hundred percent all the time. It's not impossible, it's just not likely.

Any time you make a mistake, or any time you mess up and fail, don't make it mean anything. If you fall out of integrity or fail to honor your commitments, just accept it. It happened. You might not have lived by your own personal values but that doesn't mean that you are a bad person. It doesn't mean anything. Life happens, we make a choice, we take an action, and we experience a result. Sometimes our choices move us in the direction we want to go, and sometimes they don't. The difference is how often we make choices based on our values, with integrity and commitment to who we want to be in life.

What is it that will allow you to fail, make mistakes, be out of integrity and not honor a commitment, then get back on track? How do you get moving on your goals again without losing time and focus? There are three elements. There are three things that you will have to learn and practice and put into action in your daily life.

When you do mess up, the first thing you have to do is accept what happened. Accept what happened as what you did. There is nothing you can do about it. If there is a part of you that knows you were "wrong" then it simply shows that you have values. When you have values, you'll know when you are off track.

Accept that you will fail, you will make mistakes, you will fall out of integrity and you will, on occasion, not honor your commitments. My hope for you is that from now on you do it less and less. Over time with conscious living and practicing what you are learning, you will become skillful in the art of living life as a leader. Once you become skillful in the art of living life as a leader, then you will influence others to live with that power as well. Stop giving meaning to everything and just accept life as it happens.

Second, acknowledge your mistake. Acknowledge your role and admit what you did. Acknowledge that you messed up, you made a mistake. It's okay. We all make mistakes. The trick to getting back on track quickly and living the life you want to live is doing these three things quickly.

Acknowledge that you made a mistake. Acknowledge that you broke a commitment. Acknowledge that you were out of integrity. Acknowledge that this is not who you are committed to being as a person. Acknowledge that the choice that you made does not make you a failure. You made a bad choice, that's all. You need to be able to admit that you made a mistake and you need to do this quickly. The longer you justify your mistake, the longer you try to make meaning out of it, the longer you take to just say, "I messed up," the longer you are going to allow guilt of what you did to linger on. You must acknowledge that your role in what happened was nothing more than a poor choice. It's not based on your core values and it's not who you are committed to being. It was a poor choice and it was a mistake.

The third element is, you have to communicate your mistake. That's a hard one to do. Remember, one of the hardest things to do when you make the choice to be successful is to be honest. You need to choose to be honest and choose to be open. Be honest and openly communicate what you did to the people who were affected by your choice.

You must clear up the fact that you were out of integrity with the person or persons that your decision affected. Talk to those people who were affected by your decision and acknowledge to them that you made a mistake. Apologize for being out of integrity and not honoring your commitment and then recommit to doing what you said you were going to do when you said you would do it. Clarify your expectations again and then move on. There is nothing you can do now except get back on track and do your best to live the life you want to live and live it with integrity.

By doing the steps we just talked about you can actually take your failures and turn them into an opportunity to be a positive influence. By doing these three steps you show people that you are committed to doing what you said you would do when you said you would do it. It will also show them that you're human, you're still learning, and you are willing to make these mistakes in the process.

Being willing to make mistakes, admitting them and clearing them up by recommitting to a life of integrity is a really powerful skill. When you begin doing these steps as part of who you are, you become a much more powerful person. When you start to see that you can overshadow influence, you begin to live at that other side of influence which is one of the four blocks that we talked about.

So how do you clear up what you did and practice these steps? Let's use the example of the bar/gym scenario to illustrate these points.

You call your friend and say, "I know that I influenced you to go to the bar with me last night and I'm really sorry about that. I felt bad that I made that mistake and I really want you to know that I am one hundred percent committed to our agreement and our commitment to go to the gym. I want you to know that I messed up. I didn't honor my commitment to myself, or to you, and I didn't live with integrity. I allowed the invitation to influence me to go to the bar instead of going to the gym with you and I realize that affected you as well, so I wanted to call and clear that up with you."

"I want you to know that I do want to keep our promise that we made. I want to recommit to going to the gym with you Monday through Friday. I want you to hold me accountable. I want you to make sure that if I fall off track again like I did on Friday, I want you to say, 'Wait a second, we have a commitment to each other' and I want you to hold me accountable. Can you do that for me? I'm really sorry and I hope you can understand."

Do you think this person would understand that you made a mistake, that you are committed and that you are honoring your commitment? Of course they would. So what did you do? You accepted it, you acknowledged it, and you communicated it. So when you see your co-workers on Monday you can say "Thank you so much for the invitation on Friday. I really had a good time. I really enjoyed seeing you. It was great to be with you all again. I really enjoy hanging out with you. It's one of my favorite things in the world. The reason I haven't been going and what I am really trying to avoid right now are the negative influences in my life that are keeping me from achieving my goal. You are not one of those influences but the food, the drinks and the bar are a negative influence on me. The alcohol and the food are what I'm trying to avoid, not you. I hope that you can understand that I really want to hang out with you. I really want our friendship to continue because I honor the commitment that we have in our friendship but I am just trying to avoid going to the bar and doing the happy hour thing. I'm really committed to losing these twenty pounds. It matters to me."

"If you are interested, I would like to invite you to go to the gym with us and then maybe afterwards, we could go out. There is a really delicious restaurant right next door and they serve amazing food. I'm sure you would really enjoy it. If you want to that's great, but if you don't, I understand. Please just do me a favor and don't invite me to happy hour because I'm working on overcoming those influences in my life that have caused me to gain the weight I'm working on losing. Like I said, you aren't one of them but the food and the alcohol definitely are, so I'm hoping you understand and thanks again for the invitation."

Again, what did you do? You accepted what happened. You didn't make them wrong for inviting you. You acknowledged that you made a mistake and allowed yourself to be influenced. It wasn't the people you were trying to avoid, it was the negative influences of the food and alcohol you were avoiding and you clearly communicated that to them. Then you turned that failure into an opportunity to be an influence in the lives of others. That is how you can turn what you might have viewed as a failure, into an opportunity for growth.

When you use the steps we are talking about here, you can do that. That's a powerful, and extraordinary way to live. Now you see how to reach beyond the influences in your life and start to touch the other side of what's possible. Above the level that you are at right now there is another place you can live life. That's an extraordinary place to live. You may have never experienced that place before but it's a place where you want to be. I hope you can see that just by overcoming those influences, you can start to move into that place.

Plan to have Fear

I want to talk about effective planning. Planning is going to help you overcome the other two blocks that are really going to do a good job in attempting to hold you down to this level and not allow you to break through. Effective planning requires anticipating what blocks could get in your way and devising a way to get through those blocks. Remember, in the beginning of The Next Level we said we were going to recognize the challenges but we were going to focus on the solutions. We said we were going to identify what has stopped us in the past but we are going to focus on moving forward. We also said we are going to foresee obstacles but we are going to focus on breaking through those barriers.

If you are able to plan for those obstacles, identify what has stopped you in the past, what may stop you in the future and foresee those challenges, you can find solutions quickly. You can move forward with momentum and break through those barriers that stand in your way. My focus is to make you unstoppable by preparing you for possible challenges along the way on your journey beyond these blocks, so you can respond to them more quickly. There are four specific categories that I told you about. We already identified two. The first was emotions and the second was influence.

You're already learning how to control your emotions so they don't control you. You learned how you can be bigger than influence so influence can't stand in your way. When you practice what you've learned so far, you will break through those two blocks with ferocity. You will blast through barriers on your way to living at your peak.

So what are the other two categories, what are the other two blocks that may stop you, and what are the other two blocks that you have to blast through? The third block you need to overcome is fear. We are going to focus on breaking through those barriers of fear that have been stopping you. More importantly, we're going to anticipate when they might show up and we're going to focus on breaking through those blocks of fear.

So what is your fear? Fear, is nothing more than a story. It is a story you make up based on events that have occurred in your past. Fears can arise out of your own experience or out of stories you've been told of other peoples experiences. Those stories trigger another story about what might happen in the future.

Do you have any proof at all that what has happened to you in the past and what you are fearful of will happen to you in the future? Is there any proof that just because someone else experienced something, you will too? Unless you have proof, it is a story. It's a belief. It's a perception of what you think could happen but it's not based on reality. It's a complete fabrication.

I'd like to make an example of myself right now. I've failed a lot in my life! I have wanted to be an entrepreneur for my entire life. Ever since I was a little boy, my visions of what I could achieve have been rooted in business ownership and working hard to achieve success. I have printed more business cards for ideas that never made a dime than I care to remember. My struggle for success has been a long road, but I always had an inner drive within me that kept me marching on.

Those failures in life have cost me a lot of money. They have cost me a lot of time. They have cost me a hurt, self indulged, ego and pride. Failure comes with a cost. However, if you think of failure as an investment in your success, you can focus on what you earn. Through my failure I have earned knowledge of what doesn't work. I have earned focus. I have earned courage. I have also checked my ego and pride at the door and learned thankfulness and appreciation.

I have been rejected more times than I can remember. I constantly hit my own blocks of emotion, influence and fear. Many of those blocks have stopped me in my tracks for quite a while on my journey to the peak. Nevertheless, I always found the courage to keep going, keep reaching, and keep the faith that I was on the right path to where I wanted to be. That courage is what has kept me from giving in to a life of mediocrity and longing for what could be.

Am I ever scared that I'll fail? Every day! It's that fear that I might fail that keeps me getting up early and focusing on my reason why, every day. My fear that I could leave this world without fulfilling my purpose at the highest level is what I am most afraid of in my heart.

If I made up a story that I couldn't succeed because of my previous failures, then my ultimate fear would come true. If I allowed that fear to stop me because I was afraid of the fear of rejection, then years from now I would be on death's doorstep and I would then have to look in the eyes of my children and say, "I'm really sorry, I have so much to share with you. I have so much to give but I don't have the time left. I'll give you what I have, but I allowed time to pass me by. I allowed myself to squander the time that I had and I had really big plans, I had goals, and I really wanted to leave you with something that I think would benefit your life." Do you think that the pain of rejection would hurt even a fraction of that pain of regret? Absolutely not. Fear is a story. Fear and what you are afraid of may never ever happen.

What types of fear can people have? Fear of rejection and failure are two of the biggest fears, like we just talked about. Fear of the unknown is a big one and is a huge cause of procrastination. If you don't know what's going to happen you might say, "I'm feeling kind of uneasy about this," and then you might not take any action. For sure then, your result is going to be what? Nothing. Nothing is going to change. So you will let that fear of the unknown hold you back from reaching that next level of success.

What about fear of loss? Have you been in a relationship in the past and that relationship didn't work out? If you allowed yourself to love openly and really gave of yourself then you would be heartbroken. Perhaps you decided that because of that pain you weren't going to love openly any more. You were always going to hold back. You were not going to allow the person who is in your life right now to cause you that type of pain, ever again, because you felt that in the past and you don't want to feel it again.

But let me ask you this question. Do you have any proof that the person in your life right now doesn't love you at the level that you think that they need to love you in order to live a life together forever? Do you have any proof that your relationship is going to end any time in the future? Unless you have proof, it is a story. It's a fear. It's a belief. You are allowing that fear and that story and that belief to hold you back from living a life of love at your peak.

Imagine years from now you are on death's doorstep and you are looking back at your life, at what actually happened and you say to yourself. "I never really loved. I never allowed myself to feel the love that was around me. I wasn't open. I wasn't honest. I chose to be closed off. I chose to not give fully of myself. I chose to guard my emotions and not feel love at the level I should have because I was afraid." What do you think is going to be more painful, the fear of loss, or the lost opportunity to really love?

If you did break up some time in the future, and I hope you don't, but if you did, you would have all these tools that we are learning in this book to deal with the breakup. You could say, "You know what, it happened." You would acknowledge your role in the event. If you were feeling a negative emotion, like heartbreak, which is very possible, especially during times of emotional turmoil like breakups, you would have to identify the story? What are you making it mean? Then as you continue, you can say, "You know what, I have the ability to choose what I want to feel right now. I choose to feel accepting. It happened. I don't know what this is going to lead to in my life. I have no idea what is going to happen in my future. I have no way of foreseeing what this event is going to lead to. So in this moment I'm going to choose to feel love anyway. I'm going to choose to feel happiness anyway. Instead of feeling fear and allowing fear to hold me back, I'm going to feel love and I'm going to allow love to propel me forward."

What is the opposite of fear? The opposite of fear is courage. Everyone feels fear at some level. I feel fear. I'm not going to lie and say that I am completely fearless. When you have courage, you feel the fear and you do it anyway. So if you are fearful of anything in your life, acknowledge that it is just a story. Because it is a story, you would have to allow yourself to believe something in order to continue feeling that fear and let it stop you.

In order to combat fear with courage, ask yourself this question. "In order for me to feel fear and allow it to stop me, I would have to allow myself to believe, what?" When you answer that question, you identify the story. You identify what you are allowing yourself to believe. When you believe the story you allow that fear to be a block for you. In order to overcome that fear and create courage in your life you have to say this. "Since I can now identify that my belief about what could happen is just a story, I know that I can choose to feel courageous and I choose to believe, what?" Acknowledge what you're fearful of, but acknowledge that it is just a story and create a new belief system. When you do that, when you learn to break through that block of fear, guess what happens? You start to get a little closer to the peak.

Fears – The third thing that can stop you.

I have allowed my fear of

_____

to hold me back in the past, but I am no longer going to fear those things.

I have allowed my fear of

_____

to hold me back in the past, but I am no longer going to fear those things.

I have allowed my fear of

_____

to hold me back in the past, but I am no longer going to fear those things.

Reasons

So you have started to break through the blocks of influence and you've started to break through the block of fear. You're now more in control of your emotions. What's left? What's left is breaking through the blocks of reasons.

Reasons are something that you identify as an influence and you give it a name. So, a reason might be money, or time, or energy, or ability, or lack of knowledge, or my car won't start, or I missed the bus. Whatever the influence is that you have allowed to influence your life and you give it a name, that's a reason. Since you are bigger than the influence around you, then reasons are below you. Since you play the game of life at a big level then your reasons become really small. You can crush those reasons no matter what name you give them.

Reasons, again, are nothing more than just a story. Emotions are a story. Influence is a story. Fear is a story. So I want you to identify what reasons might stop you from achieving your goals. If your goal is to run every single day and then it rains one day, are you going to allow that reason to stop you from honoring your commitment to run every day? You could. You could make the choice and know that it is just the choice that you made or you can honor your commitment and live with integrity and not let that reason stop you. Or you can create an alternate plan for exercise on the days it rains instead of skipping your exercise that day. That's powerful.

Reasons are typically called excuses. Granted, some reasons are legitimate in the short term reality of what's possible. However, history has proved that despite the challenges we face and the reasons we must overcome, there is a way. Sometimes we need to look beyond the obvious, seek wisdom and guidance and view life from a new perspective to overcome our reasons. There is a way, perhaps you just don't see it yet. But as we continue to "Advance confidently in the direction of our dreams and endeavor to live the life we have imagined," we can in fact find ourselves met with a success that we didn't expect to see.

I don't pretend to have all the answers. I understand that challenges, very strong reasons and obstacles may show up in your life. I don't know what you will personally face. I do believe, with my entire heart and soul that we are presented with all of our challenges as a test of our character. The one who creates the challenge, presents the obstacle and throws down the test in front of you has the ability to provide you with the knowledge and ability to pass the test as well. Look beyond what you see as possible and imagine what life would look like from the other side. See yourself successful and be open for the wisdom and you will have the ability to overcome any reason.

As you begin to move forward towards your goals and work on living life at the peak, identify what might stop you along the way. If you can identify your blocks, you can plan for alternative ways around those blocks. You can plan ways to get around everything so it won't stop you, it will only (possibly) slow you down.

It's not possible for possibility, fear, influence, reasons and emotions to exist in the same place. Possibility always rises above. So once you break through these blocks, possibility lies before you.

Here is the way I want you to think about the blocks in your life. I want you to think about these blocks as the enemy. You are not going to let the enemy stop you anymore. I want you to become completely unreasonable in your pursuit of the life you want to live. I want you to be an unreasonable person. There is no reason that anything should stop you, ever.

There will always be real blocks that get in our way in life. You will run into times when all four blocks can in fact stop you. However, I want you to understand the difference between the physical blocks and the psychological blocks. Both can stop you, however, both can also be overcome.

Any time you are being stopped in your life, ask yourself this question. "What would I have to believe in order to allow this to stop me?" When you find the answer, ask yourself this question. "What would I have to believe is possible in order to move beyond this block?" Followers find excuses, leaders find a way.

Reasons – The final thing that might stop you.

The reasons I've used as excuses for not

_____

are

_____

but I am not going to allow those reasons to stop me any longer!

The reasons I've used as excuses for not

_____

are

_____

but I am not going to allow those reasons to stop me any longer!

The reasons I've used as excuses for not

_____

are

_____

but I am not going to allow those reasons to stop me any longer!

Reaching Through

Imagine that you want to climb up a mountain and the bottom of that mountain is the beginning of a goal. As you start to take action you start to head up the mountain. As you make progress up the mountain you start to notice that there are clouds lingering just below the peak. You can't see the peak, but you feel like it lies just beyond the clouds. Up until now, everything was clear and it appeared like reaching the peak would be no problem. But as you get further along you start to see the clouds more clearly.

The clouds that you are seeing aren't pouring down rain, they are pouring down blocks of F.I.R.E! These clouds are dropping blocks of Fear, Influence, Reasons and Emotions. They are violent, dark and ominous looking clouds. You continue to climb that hill but the clouds keep pouring down these blocks violently upon you. Every step you take has to be carefully taken or you'll get burned. You question yourself, doubting if you can ever get through the clouds, but you have an inner belief that what you want is just beyond these blocks, through those clouds. What you want more than anything in life is just beyond the darkness.

You're looking at these clouds and saying, "It's too difficult...." But then you remember that you have been trained to get through the fire. You are a fire fighter and you need to get to the other side to rescue yourself. You remember that you have all the knowledge and tools to get to where you want to go. You may feel fear, but you have courage! You may confront a huge influence, but you are bigger than the influence! You might run into a scary reason, but you are unreasonable! You may even begin to feel every emotion you don't like to feel, but you are in control of your emotions!

At this moment, you have a choice. Are you going to allow the fear, influence, reasons or emotions to stop you from reaching the peak? Or are you going to say "NO, I'm going to get there, I'm going to get to that land of possibility that lies just beyond the clouds! I'm going to keep pushing and I am going to lead people to that place because I know it exists!"

Stop looking for people to follow in your life. Look for people who you can lead to a new land of possibility. Below those clouds is darkness. Those clouds cast shadows of doubt upon many people. You have to choose to get through those clouds and live above those clouds no matter what happens to you. When you understand the information in this book and really begin to grasp it, you are going to be able to see the light of possibility shining through the clouds as you get closer to reaching that place in your life. You are going to be less afraid to step out of that darkness and allow that light to shine upon you. You are going to grow.

You are no longer going to be afraid of how other people view you. You are going to gain that courage to grow infinitely larger. It is the moment that you step into the light of possibility that you are glorified by God and you allow yourself to be who you were born to be. At that moment, you can start to change the world, starting with yourself, starting with your own life, for the better.

We are a reflection of what's around us. If you are living in the shadows of those clouds of fear, reasons, negative emotions and influence, then what are you reflecting? You are reflecting that negativity out into the world around you. We can only shine a light of possibility when we start to reach through those clouds and reflect that light of possibility that now shines upon you. If you are stuck in the darkness of negativity, there is no light to reflect upon other people. Yet the moment you step out into that light, you reflect that light of possibility upon others.

The people you shine your brightness upon can choose to embrace that light and step up there with you. Or they might choose to retreat farther back down into that darkness because negativity is all they've ever known and they are too scared to embrace the possibility of a new life. Be that light for people. Be that hope that people want. Play the game of life big and reach beyond what you used to think was possible. Reach beyond your fear. Reach beyond your reasons. Reach beyond those influences. Reach beyond your negative emotions and allow that light of possibility to shine upon you so that you can grow larger than anything that tries to stand in your way.

It is at the moment that you say, "NO, I will no longer live in the darkness!" The moment you say "No" to those four things, you say "Yes" to yourself. You say yes to the possibility of growth in your life beyond your imagination. You must choose to step out of the shadow and step into the light. That will be a powerful and amazing moment in your life.

I'm not saying that people who don't embrace the light of possibility have horrible lives. I'm not saying that they are bad people and they live bad lives. They are just people who haven't been shown the way. I'm not here to show you how to live a good life. I'm here to show you, and it's my job, to show you how to live an extraordinary life. A life beyond what you have ever imagined possible. A life that is full of possibilities. A life full of achieved goals.

I'm going to get you there in the next section. Reaching The Peak is going to allow you to step out into that light. I'm going to show you why that is where you want to be. You do not want to live in those shadows any longer. You want to live in a world of possibility that you get to create for yourself. Be the person who breaks the chain of generations past and create a legacy of opportunity for the entire world to share.

So here is my challenge to you. I dare you. I double dog dare you. Keep going. Keep growing. Keep learning. I dare you to have the courage to take your life to the peak of what is possible. At the peak you will see your life from a whole new perspective. I'm going to show you a view of your life like you have never seen it before. I'm going to show you how to reach beyond what you see as possible and envision a life that is more extraordinary then you have ever imagined. I can and I will do my job for you. I will show you how to create and live your life as a journey of possibility. I'm going to show you a life where anything is possible, achieving your goals becomes predictable and a life where your reality becomes better than your dreams!

There are levels

There are levels to this thing called life. The higher you climb, the more clarity you find. The higher you climb, the more you want to go higher. The higher you climb, the more you begin to wonder what else there is to know, and see, and learn.

You are reaching new levels in life, but this climb is not over. This level, The Next Level, is higher than The ABC's of Success, but it's not the highest level you can reach, it's not The Peak.

The Peak is the highest level you can reach, right? Well, there is only one way to find out! Continue Your Journey Of Being, by Reaching The Peak, in the third book in this series! When you reach the peak, your understanding of life itself will be transformed!

I'll look forward to climbing with you, walking beside you, and pushing you to new realms of possibility! Come along, and see life from a whole new perspective in Your Journey Of Being – Reaching The Peak!

Made in the USA
Charleston, SC
09 December 2016